THE
DEATH
PENALTY

edited by IRWIN ISENBERG

THE REFERENCE SHELF
Volume 49   Number 2

THE H. W. WILSON COMPANY
New York   1977

THE REFERENCE SHELF

The books in this series contain reprints of articles, excerpts from books, and addresses on current issues and social trends in the United States and other countries. There are six separately bound numbers in each volume, all of which are generally published in the same calendar year. One number is a collection of recent speeches; each of the others is devoted to a single subject and gives background information and discussion from various points of view, concluding with a comprehensive bibliography. Books in the series may be purchased individually or on subscription.

HV
8694
D38

Library of Congress Cataloging in Publication Data
Main entry under title:

The Death penalty.

(The Reference shelf ; v. 49, no. 2)
Bibliography: p.
1. Capital punishment—Addresses, essays, lectures.   2. Capital punishment—United States—Addresses, essays, lectures.
I. Isenberg, Irwin.   II. Series.
HV8694.D38   364.6′6   77-23420
ISBN 0-8242-0604-5

PREFACE

On January 17, 1977, the state of Utah executed Gary Gilmore by firing squad for murder. He was the first person to be executed for a crime in the United States since 1967. For months prior to the execution, individuals and groups throughout the United States argued the pros and cons of capital punishment—and the controversy continues unabated.

In the 1950s and 1960s, increasing numbers of people spoke out against capital punishment. However, in the 1970s, as the incidence of violent crime and political terrorism increased dramatically in the United States and the world, popular feeling swung back in favor of the death penalty, which is now supported by a majority of Americans, according to recent surveys. Evidently mirroring this change in social attitude, the United States Supreme Court in 1972 made its *Furman v. Georgia* decision, which declared that many of the circumstances in which the death penalty was applied were unconstitutional. In 1976 this decision was greatly altered by the Court's ruling on *Gregg v. Georgia,* which holds that the death penalty "does not invariably violate the Constitution." It is this latter ruling that led to the Utah execution and that may provide the basis for the execution of others now on death row.

As the possibility of further executions grows, so does the national dialogue on capital punishment. Those favoring the death penalty speak of its deterrent effect on potential murderers, of society's need to protect itself, and of moral values that would seem to be twisted if the murderer is always spared while the victim's death is, of course, irrevocable.

Those who would abolish the death penalty argue that the state should not, must not, descend to barbarism

3

through official executions; that the existence of the death penalty is not really a deterrent; that the death penalty is imposed with disproportionate frequency on the poor, the uneducated, and the minorities; and that the death penalty is often handed out in an arbitrary manner. Moreover, they say, people are sometimes later found to have been innocent of the crime for which they were executed.

This volume examines the issues central to the continuing debate. These issues range far beyond the case of Gary Gilmore. What is involved are basic constitutional and legal matters, ethical and philosophic considerations, and economic and cultural questions.

The first section of this compilation surveys the status of the death penalty in the world and in the United States in particular. The section discusses the use and evolution of the death penalty through the centuries to its applications and modifications in England and America.

The second section focuses on the death penalty in the United States today. The reactions and feelings of a cross section of men on death row are presented. The implications of pertinent Supreme Court rulings are discussed and the reactions of the states to these rulings are described. In addition, the phenomenon of terrorist acts for political aims is examined.

The third section begins with two articles on Gary Gilmore, who achieved international notoriety because of his insistence that the state of Utah execute him—that it was his right to choose to die. Gary Gilmore's death wish, as it became known, resulted in fresh dispute. There follows a consideration of how the electric chair changed executions, and information on the first person to die in the electric chair and on executions occurring over such issues as slavery and the struggle to unionize.

The last section of the book reviews the arguments for and against the death penalty. It sums up the issues raised in this national debate and, in effect, asks where the reader stands.

The editor wishes to thank the publishers who have granted permission to reprint the articles in this book. He also wishes to thank Agnes Somlo for her help in compiling the volume.

IRWIN ISENBERG

May 1977

NOTE TO THE READER

For further information and an earlier perspective of historical interest, the reader is referred to Grant S. McClellan's *Capital Punishment* (Reference Shelf Series, Volume 32, Number 6) published in 1961.

CONTENTS

III. THE STATE AS EXECUTIONER

IV. LIFE OR DEATH

I. CAPITAL PUNISHMENT: PRESENT AND PAST

EDITOR'S INTRODUCTION

It is perhaps ironic that though human society through the centuries has been a more or less willing witness to indiscriminate slaughter through wars and through political, religious, and economic suppression, governments and individuals have argued long and passionately about whether it is proper to execute criminals convicted of certain crimes. A peak of some sort seems to have been reached in the twentieth century: never have so many people in so many countries been killed in wars and police-state repression; at the same time, never have so many national governments throughout the world renounced the death penalty for crimes.

The first article in this section presents a world survey of the death penalty as of the early 1970s: where it is and is not applied, for what crimes and with what frequency. There follows a review of the use of the death sentence in the United States up to the historic 1972 *Furman v. Georgia* decision, which many people thought would effectively end the use of capital punishment in this country. The article also comments on past efforts by individual states to abolish this form of punishment.

The third selection, taken from the introduction to H. A. Bedau's anthology *The Death Penalty in America*, traces the evolution of the death penalty in American criminal law from its origins in English law. It is interesting to note how, in the last few hundred years, the crimes calling for death have changed: At one point even pickpockets were executed. And, in colonial times in this country conviction for witchcraft resulted in death.

The last article speaks generally about the value of human life and asks why, if we are so troubled about using the death penalty, we should not be even more concerned about all the victims, particularly the many who die in wars or those who are killed because of negligence.

DEATH PENALTY: A WORLD SURVEY [1]

Reprinted from *U.S. News & World Report.*

Western Europe: Retreat from Execution

In all western Europe, only France and Spain still apply the death penalty in peacetime—and capital punishment appears to be on its way out in France.

Britain, after more than eight hundred years of hanging criminals, abolished the death penalty for most crimes in 1969.

Now the only offenses calling for execution in Britain are those committed in wartime—including treason, spying, and arson in naval shipyards.

Among reasons for ending the death penalty were growing doubts expressed by British criminologists, sociologists and others about the deterrent effect of capital punishment on potential criminals. The point is made that since the abolition of executions, the chances of being murdered in Britain have not increased—they remain at 3 in 1 million.

Nevertheless, public sentiment is strongly in favor of restoring the death penalty for certain crimes, such as killing policemen and children.

With crimes of violence now five times as numerous as they were twenty years ago, few people are prepared to predict that Britain has seen the last of the hangman.

In West Germany, the death penalty was ruled out by the postwar constitution adopted in 1949—largely because of revulsion against the excesses of the Nazi regime.

Over the past twenty years there have been occasional

[1] From an article in *U.S. News & World Report.* 70:38-40. My. 31, '71.

demands for reinstating executions. One demand followed a series of murders of taxi drivers in the mid-1960s. But such attempts have had no success.

In Austria, for reasons similar to those in West Germany, the death penalty was abolished by law in 1950.

On again, off again. Italy first nullified the death penalty in 1889. It was reestablished by the Fascist regime in 1926. But it was abandoned again in 1944, after Italy quit World War II. Now, Italy proposes that the United Nations prohibit death sentences in all its member countries.

Not only has Italy ended executions, it also is considering doing away with life sentences. A proposal to substitute maximum penalties of thirty to forty years' imprisonment . . . [has been under discussion for some years].

The Vatican, in 1969, canceled a forty-year-old law that decreed the death penalty for anyone attempting to assassinate the Pope within Vatican City. No execution had ever been carried out under that law.

The Netherlands repealed the death penalty in 1870, and there have been no executions in Belgium since 1863. Executions also are outlawed in Luxembourg.

The last civil execution in Switzerland was in 1940, and the death penalty was legally abolished there in 1942. Murder is rare in Switzerland. But occasionally a series of spectacular crimes involving murder has ignited movements to execute convicted killers. A parliamentary attempt to revive capital punishment was soundly beaten in the early 1950s, and the idea has not been reintroduced officially.

Switzerland, however, like several other European countries, authorizes execution by shooting in time of war as a deterrent to treason and espionage.

Trend toward discard. Although France still authorizes capital punishment, the trend there is toward presidential pardon for condemned criminals. . . .

Now the French Parliament is studying a proposal to abolish the death penalty by law. This idea appears to have popular support. A Gallup Poll in 1970 showed 58 percent of the French people opposed to the death penalty, with only 33 percent in favor. Eight years ago, a similar poll showed opinion evenly divided.

The feeling in France generally is that capital punishment is headed for the discard. [However, the capital punishment law is still on the statute books.—Ed.]

In Spain, [the late] Generalissimo Francisco Franco . . . commuted to long prison terms the death sentences of six Basque nationalists for murdering a Spanish police official. However, it was world opinion that was credited with most influencing the Franco action, rather than any popular sentiment in Spain for ending the death penalty.

Three Scandinavian countries officially gave up the death penalty before World War II—Norway in 1902, Sweden in 1921, and Denmark in 1930. In Finland, the death penalty has not been imposed in peacetime since 1826.

Scandinavians, however, hold that executions are justified for traitors who cooperate with the enemy when the very existence of a nation is threatened by foreign aggression. After World War II, Norway put to death Vidkun Quisling and about twenty others convicted either of cooperating with German occupation forces or of war crimes. Denmark executed twenty-five Danes for serving as German spies or informers.

Most Scandinavians doubt that capital punishment significantly deters crime, and its reintroduction has never been seriously suggested by any political group.

Russia: A Return to Severity

At a time when the death penalty seems to be on its way out in much of the world, the trend in Soviet Russia appears to be in the opposite direction. The Soviets reinstated capital punishment in 1950 after abolishing it in 1947.

Under Soviet law now, offenses punishable by execution include: treason, spying, crimes against the state by saboteurs, deliberate murder, rape, bribery, large-scale thefts, counterfeiting, speculation in foreign currency, and attacks on militiamen or "people's guards."

Exemptions are provided for persons under eighteen years of age and for pregnant women.

Chief culprits. Economic offenders constituted the bulk of those sentenced to death in Russia in the 1960s. According to Western intelligence sources, at least two hundred persons were executed for "economic crimes" between May 1961 and May 1963. In . . . [the first third of 1971], at least four persons were doomed to die for such crimes as theft, accepting bribes, profiteering and embezzlement.

One death sentence, for instance, was given to a former director of a state-owned machine-repair shop in Georgia. He was convicted of accepting bribes, falsifying accounts, and stealing property valued at $125,000. Another death sentence went to an ex-convict convicted by a court in Stavropol of leading a gang which stole more than $110,000 from a state-owned restaurant organization.

. . . [In December 1970] eleven persons—nine of them Jews —were convicted in Leningrad on charges of attempting to hijack an airplane in order to leave the country. Two were sentenced to die, but their sentences later were commuted to fifteen years' imprisonment—apparently as a result of a worldwide wave of anti-Soviet reaction.

Smaller toll. The death sentence still exists in Russia's Communist satellites—East Germany, Poland, Czechoslovakia, Hungary, Rumania and Bulgaria. In all these countries, however, it appears to be falling into disuse.

In Czechoslovakia, there were only 3 death sentences in 1970, compared with an average of 80 executions each year in the early 1950s. There were 2 executions in Rumania in 1968, 1 in 1969 and none in 1970. In Poland, about 60 persons were put to death in the 1960s—all for "ordinary" crimes, none for political offenses. Hungary executed between 10 and 20 persons last year.

East Germans, over the postwar years, probably have been the harshest executioners—especially in cases dealing with Nazi war crimes. From 1949 through 1967, East Germany sentenced 194 persons to death, and almost all of those sentences are believed to have been carried out. Of the total, 75 were for war crimes, 69 for crimes against the state, and the remainder for other criminal offenses.

In Yugoslavia, the number executed in the 1960s was about 5 a year, compared with 71 in 1952.

Mediterranean Area: Few Pay With Lives

Several countries on the shores of the Mediterranean have death penalties on the books for certain crimes—but they are rarely applied.

In Greece, under the . . . military dictatorship, the death penalty exists for crimes against the state—as judged by military courts. It has been more than twenty years, however, since anyone was executed. The last person sentenced to death was a man who tried to kill Premier George Papadopoulos in 1968. His sentence was reduced. [The military government ended in 1974.—Ed.]

In Turkey, capital punishment exists for serious crimes, such as premeditated murder and crimes against the state. Execution is by hanging, and one or two persons are hanged each year, on the average.

In Israel, the death penalty was abolished in 1954, with these exceptions: genocide, major crimes committed by Nazis, treason in times of actual fighting, and discharging firearms or explosives with intent to kill.

Since Israel came into existence in 1948, the only person to be executed—either in Israel proper or in territories occupied by Israel—was Adolf Eichmann, who was convicted of Nazi war crimes against the Jews.

Although, under law, many Arab terrorists captured by the Israelis could be executed, none has been or is likely to be in the near future. Military prosecutors are under specific instructions not to ask the courts for death sentences in such cases. Explaining the reason for this leniency, [Israel's] attorney general . . . says:

"Given the existing conditions, we don't think we should insert the gallows between ourselves and the Arabs as long as we can live without it. Our people understand that we shall have to live with the Arabs for some time to come."

Middle East: Death for Rebels

The death sentence, accepted by Islamic law, is common in the Arab states. Executions for civil crimes are rare. But in some countries—such as Iraq, Syria and Saudi Arabia—political unrest sometimes results in executions for treason. There is a tendency in Arab countries to use the death penalty as a deterrent to common criminals and political activists by carrying out the sentence in public. This is particularly true in Saudi Arabia, where there is no civil code and Koranic law prevails. Condemned persons are beheaded in some countries, hanged in others. [The man who assassinated Saudi Arabian King Faisal in 1975 was beheaded for his crime.—Ed.]

There has been little discussion within Arab governments over formal abolition of capital punishment. Iraq, Egypt, Syria and the Sudan all have reaffirmed the death penalty within the past five years.

Lebanon also has capital punishment, but has never used it. Public opinion in Lebanon is against executions.

Africa: A Mixed Picture

In all of the African countries south of the Sahara Desert, only two, Senegal and Mauritius, do not have the death penalty. In the Ivory Coast, Liberia and Malagasy, capital punishment exists as a matter of law, but, in actual practice, it is never carried out.

In the majority of African countries, murder and treason—interpreted to include political crimes—are punishable by death, usually by hanging or shooting.

South Africa is believed to lead the non-Communist world in the number of court-imposed executions. About 100 persons—the vast majority nonwhites—are hanged each

year. Of 97 persons executed in 1967, 2 were white; of 119
hanged in 1968, 3 were white. The death sentence is mandatory for murder. It can also be applied for treason, rape,
robbery, housebreaking, kidnapping and child-stealing.
"Sabotage" and "terrorism" committed against racial apart-
heid also can invoke death penalties.

Executions in Rhodesia are not common.

In January . . . [1971], Guinea's National Assembly
sentenced 92 persons to death by hanging for participation
in an abortive invasion by forces opposed to the government
of President Sékou Touré.

In Nigeria, executions increased to about twenty in
1970, when theft and pillage rose after the Biafran war.
[In 1967 the eastern region of Nigeria seceded, proclaim-
ing itself the Republic of Biafra. The casualties of the
civil war were estimated at over a million, many dying of
starvation in spite of international efforts to provide relief.
On January 12, 1970 the secessionists capitulated.—Ed.]

Leaders of most new countries in Africa—where political
coups are frequent—are reported reluctant to execute their
political opponents for fear of setting precedents. As a result, political plotters—though often convicted of treason—
are seldom executed.

Far East: No Easing in Sight

In no country of Asia has the death penalty been abolished—and it is not expected to disappear soon.

In military or Communist regimes, capital punishment
is considered a valuable weapon to discourage political opposition as well as common crimes.

Communist China is an extreme example of lethal punishment. Murder, rape and treason are punishable by death,
as are vaguely defined "counterrevolutionary activities."

Millions have been executed in Red China over the past
forty years—many after "public trial rallies" which are staged
without jury or defense counsel and with sentences determined beforehand. Chinese Communists in this way

wiped out almost an entire segment of society—the landlord class—just as Russians did after their revolution.

Execution also is legal in other Asian countries, including both Koreas, . . . Vietnam, and Nationalist China.

In Japan, fifteen crimes are punishable by death, including insurrection, treason, arson, murder, disrupting vital water supplies and destruction of traffic facilities that results in fatalities. Since 1945, some ten to fifteen persons have been executed each year by hanging.

Latin America: Some Relaxation

Punishment of persons convicted of major crimes varies widely in Latin America. Several countries that have capital-punishment laws on the books seldom apply them.

Brazil abolished the death penalty many years ago, but recently reinstated it for acts of terrorism. Chile retains the death penalty for murder and treason. Bolivia's maximum penalty, by law, is thirty years' imprisonment. However, in recent years, dozens of leftist guerrillas have been shot to death after having been captured. Among them was Ernesto Che Guevara, a former aide of [Cuban Premier] Fidel Castro.

Argentina abolished the death penalty in its civil code in 1922. It remains in the military-justice system, but it has been years since anyone was executed. And officials are promising to abolish all capital punishment when the country is "pacified" again.

In Mexico, the death penalty has been abolished at the national level. But most states have retained it—though it is rarely imposed. Peru and Guatemala retain capital punishment for sex crimes against children, and Guatemala also permits it for fatal kidnappings.

Canada: A Debate

Capital punishment in Canada was suspended for five years on a trial basis in 1967, but executions had all but ended long before. The last hanging was in 1962. Exceptions to the ban on execution are killers of policemen and prison guards.

Recent political terrorism has sparked renewed interest in the death penalty. A poll showed 70 percent of those surveyed favoring execution of those who kidnap persons in public life. Newspaper editorials have been critical of the commutations of about thirty death sentences since 1963. Some hold that as long as hanging remains the law, the law should be enforced.

CAPITAL PUNISHMENT IN THE U.S.: FACTS AND FIGURES [2]

Prior to 1930 no accurate statistics were maintained which reflected, on a nationwide basis, the number of persons put to death in the United States by sentence of a court of law. The earliest comprehensive records maintained by any official state agency date from the Civil War period.

In the earlier years of US history public executions were commonly held—a practice which continued in some states well into the present century. The last recorded public execution; a hanging carried out in Kentucky in 1936, was witnessed by an estimated 20,000 persons.

Executions in the United States Since 1930

In the year 1930, 155 persons were executed in the United States, a figure which rose in the middle 1930s to a level of approximately 200 per year for a brief period, then showed a steady decline to the middle 1960s. In 1966, one person was executed, and in 1967—the last year in which an execution took place—2 persons were put to death.

Over the period from 1930 to 1967 there were 3,859 recorded executions in the United States. Most of these— 3,335—were for murder. In addition, there were 455 execu-

[2] From "Controversy Over the Question of Capital Punishment in the U.S." *Congressional Digest.* 52:2-4. Ja. '73. Reprinted by permission.

tions for rape, 24 for armed robbery, 20 for kidnapping, 11 for burglary, 6 for aggravated assault by prisoners serving life sentences, and 8 for the federal crime of espionage.

Thirty-three of these 3,859 persons were executed as violators of federal statutes (including the eight espionage cases cited); the remainder were capital offenders under state laws. The above totals, it should be noted, do not include 160 executions by the US armed forces for murder, rape, and—in one case—desertion.

The decline in executions is evident in following annual averages, beginning with the decade of 1930-39. In that period, the annual average was 166; in the 1940s, 127; in the 1950s, 71. Federal executions follow a generally comparable trend, with 10 in the 1930s, a rise to 13 per year on the average in the 1940s, 9 in the 1950s, and 1 only during all of the 1960s (in 1963).

Historically, a variety of methods have been employed in the execution of criminals. In the modern era, however, the three methods of execution universally employed have been electrocution, lethal gas, and hanging, although state law in Utah also authorizes execution by shooting.

Death Row Population

The moratorium on executions nationwide, which became effective in mid-1967 after a series of successful "abolitionist" activities, did not serve to suspend the imposition of the death sentence. While some courts and juries were doubtless influenced by developments which had brought about the cessation of executions pending a Supreme Court determination on pending cases, the conviction and sentencing of capital offenders continued in the five-year period between the last execution in 1967 and the Supreme Court's *Furman* decision in mid-1972 . . . outlawing use of the death penalty as it was applied under most statutes. [At that time] there were 631 persons awaiting execution in 32 states. All of these but 2 were men. Racially there were 267 whites, 351 blacks, and 13 "others." By offenses, 547 of the condemned had been convicted for murder, 80 for rape, and 4 for armed robbery.

By states, the death row populations at the time of the *Furman* decision were as follows:

Alabama, 31; Arizona, 19; Arkansas, 6; Colorado, 2; Connecticut, 3; Delaware 3; District of Columbia 3; Florida, 102 (including one woman); Georgia, 42; Illinois, 31; Indiana, 9; Kansas, 2; Kentucky, 21; Louisiana, 48; Maryland, 23; Massachusetts, 23; Mississippi, 9; Missouri, 16; Nebraska, 2; Nevada, 8; New Hampshire, 2; New York, 5; North Carolina, 11; Ohio, 63; Oklahoma, 15; Pennsylvania, 26 (including one woman); South Carolina, 11; Tennessee, 16; Texas, 52; Utah, 5; Virginia, 12; Washington, 10.

California's earlier substantial death row population is not reflected in the above figures, since the action of that state's supreme court in February 1972 overturning the death penalty had resulted in the commutation of sentences for all prisoners condemned to death. A similar situation applies in the case of New Jersey . . .

Before Furman

In recent years a major effort has been mounted by opponents of capital punishment to seek abolition of the death penalty in the United States. Long an accepted form of punishment for serious or "capital" offenses under federal law and that of most of the states, the putting to death of convicted offenders has been attacked intermittently since the early nineteenth century by a succession of individuals and organizations opposed to the practice.

While some past efforts have been concentrated on the federal government in the belief that accomplishing repeal of federal capital-punishment statutes would set an example which state governments would follow, the main thrust of most efforts until the past decade has remained at the state level. Virtually all of the common "capital" offenses are defined and principally punished by the individual states.

. . . Federally-defined capital offenses are, with few exceptions, somewhat uncommon in nature.

Abolitionist efforts in the United States were successful in several jurisdictions in the early nineteenth century. Among the first political entities in the world to abolish capital punishment were the states of Michigan (which acted in 1846), Rhode Island (1852), and Wisconsin (1853). For more than a half-century following these actions the abolitionist effort languished, but in the decade between 1907 and 1917 ten states abolished the death penalty for murder (although by 1919 five of these had reintroduced it).

The next significant period in the anti-capital-punishment movement in the United States did not arrive until the years following World War II—most particularly, the decade of the 1960s and early 1970s.

In this period six states abolished the death penalty, with few or no qualifications: Oregon in 1964; West Virginia, Vermont, Iowa, and New York in 1965; and New Mexico in 1969. Also during this decade the last mandatory death penalties for first degree murder were repealed —in the District of Columbia in 1962 and New York in 1963. These were replaced by optional death sentences at the discretion of a jury.

At the same time that efforts to suspend or abolish capital punishment were making headway on both legislative and judicial fronts, several new categories of crime were classed as capital offenses. At the federal level, air piracy was so designated in 1961 and assassination of the President or Vice President in 1964. In 1970 the state of California provided the death penalty for anyone exploding a "destructive device" which caused great harm or injury.

"Abolition" in the Courts

In 1967 the appearance of the report of the National Crime Commission coincided with renewed efforts by opponents of capital punishment to secure the suspension of executions while a series of cases that had been appealed

to the United States Supreme Court were under consideration.

A major device in this campaign was the class action
suit, a number of which were initiated by NAACP [Na-
tional Association for the Advancement of Colored People]
Legal Defense Fund attorneys. These were successful in
blocking executions in Florida and, subsequently, California. These actions, in turn, had the effect of halting
other executions pending judicial determination of "due
process" and "equal protection" issues which had been
raised in such cases against state death sentences for murder,
rape, and other crimes. The following year, 1968, was the
first in which no execution occurred under American civil
law.

These initial efforts to abolish capital punishment
through concentrated judicial action had, as noted, been
based on "due process" and "equal protection" questions
arising principally from allegations of racial and economic
discrimination in the application of the death penalty.

In 1969 the Supreme Court heard argument for the first
time that the death penalty is unconstitutional under the
Eighth Amendment, which prohibits "cruel and unusual
punishments." In the case of *Boykin v. Alabama* the Court
reversed a death penalty conviction for robbery, but on
grounds other than those being argued.

In the following year the first of several actions occurred
which were to have major impact on the use of capital
punishment. In December 1970, a United States Court of
Appeals held that the death penalty for rape violated the
Eighth Amendment's cruel and unusual punishments prohibition where the victim's life was neither taken nor endangered. This finding was regarded as judicially historic
in that it was the first time an appellate court had found
a capital statute to be in violation of the "cruel and unusual punishments" proscription.

During the same month, . . . Governor Winthrop Rockefeller of Arkansas commuted the sentences of all fifteen men

then under sentence of death in his state. In a public statement, Governor Rockefeller indicated his hope that his position and action would "have an influence on other governors."

In January 1971 the National Commission on Reform of Federal Criminal Laws, chaired by former Governor of California Edmund G. Brown, issued its report, which included a recommendation that all federal capital punishment statutes be abolished. At approximately the same time the Pennsylvania attorney general declared that the death penalty in his state was unconstitutional, and ordered the state's electric chair dismantled.

Background of Supreme Court Furman *Decision*

By the time a divided United States Supreme Court handed down its 5-4 decision in 1972 in the case of *Furman v. Georgia,* approximately one-fifth of the states had abolished capital punishment. As of March 1972, three months prior to the *Furman* decision, 39 states retained the death penalty, generally for first degree murder, although five of these limited its imposition to exceptional cases involving such offenses as murder of a police officer or prison guard, or for second-offense murderers. [Two others, California and New Jersey, abolished the death penalty just before the *Furman* decision.—Ed.] Most capital punishment jurisdictions punished the same general categories of crime with death—most commonly, murder, rape, and armed robbery—although one state, Alabama, named as many as seventeen capital offenses in its statutes.

In the light of the reasoning which emerged in the *Furman* decision, it is of note that in every jurisdiction which retained capital punishment its imposition was discretionary rather than mandatory for all but a few specified crimes in several states.

Several decisions of the Supreme Court handed down in the post–World War II years have had significant effect on the efforts of both proponents and opponents of capital punishment. Among the more . . . frequently cited in debate over the subject are:

Louisiana ex rel Francis v. Resweber (1946), in which it was stated that "the cruelty against which the Constitution protects a convicted man is cruelty inherent in the method of punishment, not the necessary suffering involved in any method humanely employed to extinguishing life humanely."

United States v. Jackson (1967), in which the Court held that the death penalty provision of the Federal Kidnapping Act (the "Lindbergh Act") was invalid because the procedures for imposing it heavily favored a guilty plea or jury waiver.

Witherspoon v. Illinois (1968), in which it was found unconstitutional to exclude jurors who admitted to qualms concerning imposition of the death penalty.

McGautha v. California (1971), and others, in which the Court held that due process did not require that juries authorized to impose the death sentence be guided by any established standards in the exercise of their discretion, and stated, in effect, that the Court would not further pursue . . . the objection that the death penalty is in violation of the Fourteenth Amendment's "equal protection" clause.

The California Decision

On February 18, 1972, the California supreme court issued an opinion in the case of *People v. Anderson* which quickly received national attention. Holding that the imposition of the death penalty as practiced in California was violative of that state's constitution, the court set forth its salient conclusion in the following:

A jury found Robert Page Anderson guilty of first degree murder, the attempted murder of three men, and first degree robbery, and fixed the penalty at death for the murder. The judgment was affirmed. Thereafter . . . the judgment was reversed insofar as it related to the death penalty under the compulsion of *Witherspoon v. Illinois.* . . .

A second trial was had on the issue of the penalty for the

murder, and the jury again imposed the death penalty. A motion
for a new trial was denied, and this appeal is now before us automatically [under provisions of the California Penal Code].

Defendant contends that error was committed in selecting
the jury, that certain evidence was improperly admitted, that the
prosecutor was guilty of prejudicial misconduct, and that the
death penalty constitutes both cruel and unusual punishment
and, as such, contravenes the Eighth Amendment to the United
States Constitution and Article I, Section 6, of the constitution of
California. We have concluded that capital punishment is both
cruel and unusual as those terms are defined under Article I,
Section 6, of the California constitution, and that therefore death
may not be exacted as punishment for crime in this state. Because we have determined that the California constitution does
not permit the continued application of capital punishment, we
need not consider whether capital punishment may also be proscribed by the Eighth Amendment to the United States Constitution. [For a discussion of later rulings and their effects, see
"New Life for the Death Penalty," by H. A. Bedau, in Section II,
below.—Ed.]

EVOLUTION OF THE DEATH PENALTY IN AMERICA [3]

American criminal law was not created out of nothing
by the original colonists and the Founding Fathers. Rather,
it took its shape directly from English criminal law of the
sixteenth, seventeenth and eighteenth centuries. In order to
appreciate the structure that this tradition imparted to the
American law of capital punishment, it is necessary to review, if only briefly, the experience in England with the
death penalty during our nation's formative years. . . .

Capital Punishment in England and America: "The Bloody Code"

By the end of the fifteenth century, English law recognized eight major capital crimes: treason (including at-

[3] From the Introduction to *The Death Penalty in America; an Anthology,*
edited by Hugo Adam Bedau, Doubleday. rev ed p i-xxii. '67. Copyright ©
1964, 1967 by Hugo Adam Bedau. Reprinted by permission of Doubleday & Company, Inc.

tempts and conspiracies), petty treason (killing of a husband
by his wife), murder (killing a person with "malice"), lar-
ceny, robbery, burglary, rape and arson. Under the Tudors
and Stuarts [royal families of England], many more crimes
entered this category. By 1688 there were nearly fifty. During the reign of George II, nearly three dozen more were
added, and under George III the total was increased by
sixty. The highpoint was reached shortly after 1800. One
estimate put the number of capital crimes at 223 as late as
1819. It is impossible to detail here the incredible variety
of offenses involved. Crimes of every description against the
state, against the person, against property, against the public peace were made punishable by death. Even with fairly
lax enforcement after 1800, between two thousand and
three thousand persons were sentenced to death each year
from 1805 to 1810.

Conviction of a capital offense, whether or not sentence
was executed, resulted in attainder: forfeiture of all lands
and property, and denial of all right of inheritance ("cor-
ruption of blood"). Although appeal of the death sentence
itself to a higher tribunal was all but impossible, the de-
scendants of an executed criminal occasionally succeeded
in appealing the attainder.

The usual mode of execution was hanging, though there
were several crimes for which this was deemed insufficient.
The bodies of pirates were hung in chains from specially
built gibbet irons along the wharves of London. Throughout England, the rotting corpses of executed criminals dot-
ted the countryside, a grim warning to other malefactors.
Executions were always conducted in public and often became the scene of drunken revels. Thackeray's vivid description is famous; he wrote in part:

I must confess . . . that the sight has left on my mind an extraordinary feeling of terror and shame. It seems to me that I have
been abetting an act of frightful wickedness and violence, performed by a set of men against one of their fellows; and I pray
God that it may soon be out of the power of any man in England

to witness such a hideous and degrading sight. Forty thousand persons (say the Sheriffs), of all ranks and degrees—mechanics, gentlemen, pickpockets, members of both Houses of Parliament, street-walkers, newspaper-writers, gather together before Newgate at a very early hour: the most part of them give up their natural quiet night's rest in order to partake of this hideous debauchery, which is more exciting than sleep, or than wine, or the last new ballet, or any other amusement they can have . . .

Traitors, whether guilty of petty or high treason, were subject to especially aggravated forms of execution. Burning to death was the fate of many a woman convicted of killing her husband. As late as 1786, a crowd of thousands watched as one Phoebe Harris was burned at the stake. But the worst punishment was reserved for criminals guilty of high treason. When Sir Walter Raleigh touched the headsman's sword, he is supposed to have quipped, " 'Tis a sharp medicine." Beheading was the least of it. The standard practice, according to the great authority on English law, Sir William Blackstone, consisted of drawing, hanging, disemboweling, and then beheading, followed by quartering. In 1812, this death sentence was pronounced in England on seven men convicted of high treason:

That you and each of you, be taken to the place from whence you came, and from thence be drawn on a hurdle to the place of execution, where you shall be hanged by the neck, not till you are dead; that you be severally taken down, while yet alive, and your bowels be taken out and burnt before your faces—that your heads be then cut off, and your bodies cut into four quarters, to be at the King's disposal. And God have mercy on your souls.

This "bloody code," . . . with its scores of capital offenses and almost daily public executions, was considerably mitigated by benefit of clergy and the Royal prerogative of mercy. Benefit of clergy arose from the struggle between church and state in England, and it originally provided that priests, monks and other clerics were to be remanded from secular to ecclesiastical jurisdiction for trial on indictment of felony. In later centuries, this privilege was applied in ordinary criminal courts to more and more persons and for an ever larger number of felonies. Eventually, all persons accused of capital crimes were spared a death sentence if the crime was a first felony offense and if it was clergyable, provided only the criminal could recite the "Neck verse" (the opening lines of Psalm LI), this being construed by the court as proof of his literate (and thus clerical) status. Benefit of clergy became in effect the fictional device whereby first offenders were given a lesser punishment.

A far different practice having a comparable effect was the trial court's frequent recommendation to the Crown that mercy be granted. Such recommendations were natural enough, since the judge had no alternative upon the conviction of an accused but to sentence him to death; all felonies carried a mandatory death penalty. Because the court's plea for mercy was usually granted (even during the years when Parliament was increasing the number of capital crimes!), hundreds of persons convicted and sentenced to death were not executed. Instead, they were transported to the colonies. During the last decade of the eighteenth century, in London and Middlesex alone, more than two-thirds of all death sentences were reversed through the Royal prerogative of mercy. Although death sentences issued annually throughout England sometimes ran in the thousands, by the 1800s executions apparently never exceeded seventy. . . .

The American colonies had no uniform criminal law. The range of variation during the seventeenth and eighteenth centuries, so far as capital punishment is concerned, was considerable. It may be gauged from the differences in the penal codes of Massachusetts, Pennsylvania, and North Carolina. The earliest recorded set of capital statutes on these shores are those of the Massachusetts Bay Colony, dating from 1636. This early codification, titled "The Capitall Lawes of New-England," lists in order the following crimes: idolatry, witchcraft, blasphemy, murder . . . , assault in sudden anger, sodomy, buggery, adultery, statutory rape,

rape (punishment of death optional), man-stealing, perjury in a capital trial, and rebellion (including attempts and conspiracies). Each of these crimes was accompanied in the statute with an Old Testament text as its authority. How rigorously these laws were enforced is not known. . . .

In later decades, this theocratic criminal code gave way in all but a few respects to purely secular needs. Before 1700, arson and treason, as well as the third offense of theft of goods valued at over forty shillings, were made capital, despite the absence of any biblical justification. By 1785, the Commonwealth of Massachusetts recognized nine capital crimes, and they bore only slight resemblance to the thirteen "Capitall Lawes" of the Bay Colony: treason, piracy, murder, sodomy, buggery, rape, robbery, arson and burglary.

Far milder than the Massachusetts laws were those adopted in South Jersey and Pennsylvania by the original Quaker colonists. The Royal charter for South Jersey in 1646 did not prescribe the death penalty for any crime, and there was no execution in this colony until 1691. In Pennsylvania, William Penn's Great Act of 1682 specifically confined the death penalty to the crimes of treason and murder. These ambitious efforts to reduce the number of capital crimes were defeated early in the eighteenth century when the colonies were required to adopt, at the direction of the Crown, a far harsher penal code. By the time of the War of Independence, many of the colonies had roughly comparable capital statutes. Murder, treason, piracy, arson, rape, robbery, burglary, sodomy, and, from time to time, counterfeiting, horse-theft, and slave rebellion—all were usually punishable by death. Benefit of clergy was never widely permitted, and hanging was the usual method of inflicting the death penalty.

Some states, however, preserved a severer code. As late as 1837, North Carolina required death for all the following crimes: murder, rape, statutory rape, arson, castration, burglary, highway robbery, stealing bank notes, slave-steal-

ing, "the crime against nature" (buggery, sodomy, besti-
ality), duelling if death ensues, burning a public building,
assault with intent to kill, breaking out of jail if under a
capital indictment, concealing a slave with intent to free
him, taking a free Negro or mulatto out of the state with
intent to sell him into slavery; the second offense of forgery,
mayhem, inciting slaves to insurrection, or of circulating
seditious literature among slaves; being an accessory to
murder, robbery, burglary, arson, or mayhem. Highway
robbery and bigamy, both capitally punishable, were also
clergyable. This harsh code persisted so long in North
Carolina partly because the state had no penitentiary and
thus had no suitable alternative to the death penalty.

The Movement for Reform

In England, the first of hundreds of capital statutes to
be repealed early in the last century was a law enacted in
1565 which made picking pockets a capital offense; it was
abolished in 1810 "without opposition or comment." Penal
reform in America dates from about the same period, and
was inspired by the same continental thinkers who stimulated reform in England. In May 1787, Dr. Benjamin Rush
(1745–1813) gave a lecture in Benjamin Franklin's house
in Philadelphia to a group of friends, recommending the
construction of a "House of Reform," a penitentiary, so
that criminals could be taken off the streets and detained
until purged of their antisocial habits. A little over a year
later, Rush followed this lecture with an essay, entitled
"Inquiry into the Justice and Policy of Punishing Murder
by Death." He argued its impolicy and injustice. This essay, published a few years later, became the first of several
memorable pamphlets originating in this country to urge
the cause of abolition, and Dr. Rush is usually credited
with being the father of the movement to abolish capital
punishment in the United States.

Rush's argument was based on the analysis originating
with the Italian jurist, Cesare Beccaria, whose book, *On*

Crimes and Punishments, had been published a generation earlier and had stirred all European intellectuals. The main points of Rush's argument were simple enough: scriptural support for the death penalty was spurious; the threat of hanging does not deter but increases crime; when a government puts one of its citizens to death, it exceeds the powers entrusted to it. In the years immediately following the publication of Rush's essay, several other prominent citizens in Philadelphia, notably Franklin and the attorney general, William Bradford, gave their support to reform of the capital laws. In 1794, they achieved the repeal of the death penalty for all crimes in Pennsylvania except for the crime of "first degree" murder.

These reforms in Pennsylvania had no immediate influence in other states. . . . In the United States no major public figures emerged as leaders in this movement until several decades later. The most distinguished American lawyer in this group was Edward Livingston (1764–1836). Under commission from the Louisiana legislature, and inspired by the radical approach to crime and punishment being preached with such persuasiveness in France and England, Livingston prepared a revolutionary penal code for Louisiana. At the center of his proposals, he insisted, was "the total abolition of capital punishment." The legislature was not convinced, and it rejected most of his recommendations, including this one. Livingston did not live long enough to learn that during the next half-century, the leading piece of anti-capital-punishment propaganda in the United States was a thirty-page excerpt from his model Louisiana code.

Not until the 1830s did the literary efforts of Rush and Livingston begin to bear fruit. By this time, the legislatures in several states (notably Maine, Massachusetts, Ohio, New Jersey, New York and Pennsylvania) were besieged each year with petitions on behalf of abolition from their constituents. Special legislative committees were formed to receive these messages, hold hearings, and submit recommendations. Anti-gallows societies came into being in every state along the eastern seaboard, and in 1845 an American Society for the Abolition of Capital Punishment was organized. With the forces arrayed against slavery and saloons, the anti-gallows societies were among the most prominent groups struggling for social reform in America.

The highwater mark was reached in the later 1840s, when Horace Greeley, the editor and founder of the New York *Tribune,* became one of the nation's leading critics of the death penalty. In New York, Massachusetts, and Pennsylvania, abolition bills were constantly before the legislature. Then, in 1846, the Territory of Michigan voted to abolish hanging and to replace it with life imprisonment for all crimes save treason. This law took effect on March 1, 1847, and Michigan became the first English-speaking juris-diction in the world to abolish the death penalty, for all practical purposes. In 1852, Rhode Island abolished the gallows for all crimes, including treason; the next year Wisconsin did likewise. In several other states, capital pun-ishment for many lesser crimes was replaced by life im-prisonment, and other reforms affecting the administration of the death penalty were adopted. By the middle of the . . . [nineteenth] century in most of the northern and eastern states, only treason and murder universally remained as capitally punishable crimes. Few states outside the South had more than one or two additional capital offenses. The anti-gallows movement rapidly lost its momentum, how-ever, as the moral and political energies of the nation be-came increasingly absorbed in the struggle over slavery.

After the Civil War and the Reconstruction Era, both Iowa and Maine abolished the death penalty, only to re-store it promptly. In 1887, Maine again abolished it, thereby becoming the only American jurisdiction which has twice voted to end the death penalty. During this pe-riod, the federal government, after extensive debate in Congress, did reduce its dozens of capital crimes to three: murder, treason and rape (and for none was death mandatory). Colorado abolished the death penalty for a few years, but reinstated it in the face of what at the time seemed the threat of mob rule. In that state, public dissatisfaction with mere imprisonment twice resulted in lynchings during the abolition years.

Between the peak of the Progressive Era and the years when women got the vote and whiskey got the gate, no less than eight states—Kansas, Minnesota, Washington, Oregon, North and South Dakota, Tennessee, and Arizona—abolished the death penalty for murder and for most other crimes. In only a few states did the reform last, however. By 1921, Tennessee, Arizona, Washington, Oregon and Missouri had reinstated it. During the Prohibition Era, when law enforcement often verged on total collapse, the abolitionists were nearly routed in several states. Had it not been for the persuasive voices of Clarence Darrow, the great "attorney for the damned," and of Lewis E. Lawes, the renowned warden of Sing Sing Prison, and the organization in 1927 of the American League to Abolish Capital Punishment, the lawless era of the twenties might have seen the death penalty reintroduced in every state in the Union.

Throughout this period in England, the abolition movement remained somewhat more popular. . . . A select committee of the House of Commons studied the issue and published a scholarly report in 1931. Although they recommended an experimental period of five years without the death penalty, no action was taken by the government. Immediately after the end of World War II, while the Labor party controlled the government, several Labor M.P.s struggled to have their party vote out the death penalty, as abolition was one of the social reforms that labor and socialist parties in many countries had promised for decades. Even so, the government was not receptive. As a compromise measure it created in 1949 a Royal Commission on Capital Punishment, which was expressly forbidden to consider whether the death penalty should be abolished.

Nevertheless, it was this Commission's investigations, stretching over four years, which set off . . . [a] wave of agitation against the death penalty in the Commonwealth countries and in the United States.

It was quite clear that the Royal Commissioners favored complete abolition as the best solution to the complex legal and penal problems they were forced to face, even though their explicit recommendations . . . were required to fall short of this radical position. No sooner was their report published than the Canadian Parliament established its own inquiry into capital punishment, and several United States experts gave testimony at these hearings. Concurrently, debates at the United Nations often touched on the compatibility of the state's right to kill and the individual's right to live. Many of the delegates, especially the Scandinavian, Benelux [Belgium, the Netherlands and Luxembourg], and Latin American representatives, were from nations that had long abandoned recourse to the executioner in peace time. Thus it was that several American organizations, notably the Society of Friends and the American League to Abolish Capital Punishment, were encouraged to restimulate public interest against the death penalty in the United States as well.

By the later 1950s, abolition groups were once again active and moderately well organized in nearly two dozen death penalty states in this country. Public hearings on abolition bills were again echoing in legislative chambers, reminiscent of the 1840s and 1910s. Although intensive efforts in California and Massachusetts failed to obtain repeal of the death penalty, they did achieve legislative committee reports recommending abolition. Rather unnoticed, both Alaska and Hawaii, while still territories, eliminated the death penalty in 1957. Not noticed at all was the 1952 constitutional provision in the Commonwealth of Puerto Rico forbidding the death penalty for any crime. The signal triumph at this time was in Delaware, where, in April 1958 all the state's capital laws were repealed. During 1960 and 1961, both Ohio and Pennsylvania issued legislative committee reports favoring an end to capital punishment. The movement suffered a considerable and unexpected defeat, however, when Delaware suddenly restored the death penalty for murder late in 1961. . . .

Methods of Execution

The variety of ways in which men have put one another to death under the law is appalling. History records such exotic practices (fortunately, largely unknown in the Anglo-American tradition) as flaying and impaling, boiling in oil, crucifixion, pulling asunder, breaking on the wheel, burying alive, and sawing in half. But not so many generations ago, in both England and America, criminals were occasionally pressed to death, drawn and quartered, and burned at the stake. Had any of these punishments survived the eighteenth century, there is little doubt that public reaction would have forced an end to capital punishment long ago.

Originally, the purpose of *peine forte et dure* (pressing to death) was to force an accused person to plead to an indictment. Such tactics became necessary because anyone who refused to plead to a felony indictment (that is, refused to plead either guilty or innocent) could avoid forfeiture even if he was later found guilty. The effect of pressing on an uncooperative accused was, and was intended to be, fatal. As early as 1426, pressing was used in England, though it never seems to have enjoyed wide popularity with the courts. Its sole recorded use in this country seems to have been during the notorious Salem [Massachusetts] witchcraft trials, in 1692, when one Giles Cory was pressed to death for refusal to plead to the charge of witchcraft.

Burning at the stake is intimately connected with the punishment of witchcraft and heresy, having been endorsed for these crimes by several medieval Christian theologians. In civilized countries, such as England, . . . it was the practice to strangle the condemned person before the flames

reached him. There are records showing that in New York
and New Jersey, and probably elsewhere in the American
colonies, rebellious Negro slaves were burned at the stake
during the early and middle eighteenth century. Except
for these occasional excesses, however, burning at the stake
seems to have played no part among standard methods of
execution actually practiced on these shores.

It is somewhat curious that any of these barbarous and
inhumane methods of execution survived as long as they
did, for the English Bill of Rights of 1689 proscribed "cruel
and unusual punishments." This phrase worked its way
through several of the early American state constitutions
into the federal Bill of Rights (in the Eighth Amendment)
of 1789. Supreme Court opinions interpreting this clause
have been few, but they agree in declaring that the intent
of the Framers of the Constitution was to rule out, once
and for all, the aggravations attendant on execution, e.g.,
drawing and quartering, pressing, or burning. These practices had all but totally disappeared by 1789 and they had
never taken firm root here, anyway; but their express ex-
clusion by Jefferson, Madison and the other authors of the
Bill of Rights was a service to the interests of a free and
humane people. Except when executing spies, traitors and
deserters, who could be shot under martial law, the sole
acceptable mode of execution in the United States for a
century after the adoption of the Eighth Amendment was
hanging.

In the 1880s, as one story has it, in order to fight the
growing success of General Electric Company, which was
pressing for nationwide electrification with alternating current, the advocates of direct current staged public demon-
strations to show how dangerous their competitor's product
really was: if it could kill animals—and awed spectators
saw that, indeed, it could—it could kill human beings as
well. Within a few years, this somber warning was turned
completely around, and in 1880, the New York legislature
approved the dismantling of its gallows and the construc-

tion of an "electric chair," on the theory that in all respects, scientific and humane, executing a condemned man by electrocution was superior to executing him by hanging. On June 27, 1893, after his lawyer had unsuccessfully argued the unconstitutionality of this "unusual" method of execution, one William Kemmler became the first criminal to be put to death by electricity. Although the execution was little short of torture for Kemmler (the apparatus was makeshift and the executioner clumsy), the fad had started. Authorities on electricity, such as Thomas Edison and Nikola Tesla, continued to debate whether electrocution was so horrible that it never should have been invented. The late Robert G. Elliot, electrocutioner of 387 men and women, assured the public in his memoirs that the condemned man loses consciousness immediately with the first jolt of current. The matter remains controversial to this day. Despite the record of bungled executions, the unavoidable absence of first-hand testimony, and the invariable odor of burning flesh that accompanies every electrocution, most official observers favor the electric chair. However ironical it may be, it is a fact that electrocution was originally adopted and is still employed in two dozen states on the grounds of its superiority to hanging as a civilized method of killing criminals.

Not satisfied with shooting, hanging or electrocution, the Nevada legislature passed a bill in 1921 to provide that a condemned person should be executed in his cell, while asleep and without any warning, with a dose of lethal gas. Governor Emmet Boyle, an avowed opponent of capital punishment, signed the bill, confident that it would be declared unconstitutional on the grounds of "cruel and unusual punishment." Nothing much was done one way or the other until one Gee Jon was found guilty of murder and sentenced to death. When the Nevada supreme court upheld the constitutionality of lethal gas, a chamber was hurriedly constructed after practical obstacles were discovered in the original plan for holding the execution in the prisoner's cell. On February 8, 1924, Jon became the first person to be legally executed with a lethal dose of cyanide gas. . . .

In this country, voices are occasionally still heard, protesting the risks, indignities and mutilations incident on hangings, shootings, electrocutions and gassings. "Contemporary methods of execution," it has been said, "are unnecessarily cruel"; they are "archaic, inefficient, degrading for everyone involved." Novelties, such as allowing the condemned man to choose the method of his execution, or even to administer it to himself, or to become the subject of medical experiments until he dies of a fatal one, have . . . been suggested. But these objections and suggestions seem to go almost entirely unheeded. Retentionists—those who favor keeping, adopting or extending the death penalty—usually have no curiosity about the regrettable details of actual executions, and abolitionists, being totally out of sympathy with the whole business, have no interest in finding a more humane way to do what they disapprove of on principle.

Private Executions

The strongest argument in favor of public executions and of cruel methods of inflicting the death penalty was that such procedures greatly increased the deterrent effect. Hence, the desirability of having children and the criminal fringe of society witness these spectacles. . . . It was probable . . . [however], that the deterrent effect of attending an execution was considerably overrated. A classic tale has it that when pickpocketing was a capital crime in England, pickpockets plied their trade at the foot of the gallows while the other spectators watched a pickpocket being hanged! . . .

Public executions continued well into the last century . . . until New York, in 1830, imposed some control on the county sheriffs, requiring them (but only at their discretion!) to hold executions away from public view. Not until

1835 did New York increase the stringency of this law so as to prohibit public executions. Within the next few years, several other states followed suit, and this reform—at most, merely a sop to abolitionists—was underway.

The reform was by no means universal or thorough-going, however. Pennsylvania and New Jersey, for instance, stipulated only that executions should take place within the walls or buildings of the county jail. Since in most cases the gallows was erected out of doors in the jail yard, it was a simple enough matter for any interested spectator to watch the entire proceeding from a vantage point well outside the walls. Not until nearly the end of the last century were such abuses prohibited. Even so, flagrantly public executions continued in some states until quite recently. The last such event in the United States is said to have been the hanging of a Negro in Owensboro, Kentucky, in August 1936. A news service photograph taken moments after the "drop" shows some 20,000 people packed around the gallows, with the dead man dangling at the end of his rope. Several spectators are atop a nearby utility pole, and others are leaning out of windows a block away. The platform is jammed with official witnesses. Two years later, Kentucky passed a statute prohibiting all but official witnesses from attending future executions.

Even . . . [in the 1960s] however, most states . . . [allowed] considerable discretion to the warden in charge of an execution as to how many persons . . . qualify as official guests and witnesses. Wardens and executioners have often told how the announcement of an execution (required by law) brings a flood of requests for permission to attend. Such requests, they say, are never granted. But if the condemned man is enough of a celebrity, the mass news media will send their representatives, and these, plus the officials directly and indirectly involved, often swell the total to several dozen, as in the execution of Julius and Ethel Rosenberg [convicted of treason] at Sing Sing in 1953 and

of Caryl Chessman [convicted of murder] at San Quentin in
1960.

ABOVE AND BEYOND
CAPITAL PUNISHMENT [4]

[James] Boswell to [Samuel] Johnson . . . [in a letter written in 1777]:

You have said nothing to me of Dr. Dodd. I know not how
you think on that subject; though the newspapers give us a saying
of yours in favour of mercy to him. But I own I am very desirous
that the royal prerogative of remission of punishment should be
employed to exhibit an illustrious instance to the regard which
God's Viceregent will ever show to piety and virtue. If for ten
righteous men the Almighty would have spared Sodom, shall not
a thousand acts of goodness done by Dr. Dodd counterbalance
one crime?

Johnson to Boswell . . .

Poor Dodd was put to death yesterday, in opposition to the
recommendation of the jury, the petition of the city of London,
and a subsequent petition signed by three-and-twenty-thousand
hands. Surely the voice of the public, when it calls so loudly and
calls only for mercy, ought to be heard.

The saying that was given me in the papers I never spoke,
but I wrote many of his petitions and some of his letters. He was,
I am afraid, long flattered with hopes of life; but I had no part
in the dreadful delusion, for as soon as the King had signed his
sentence, I obtained . . . an account of the disposition of the
court towards him, with a declaration that there was no hope
even of a respite.

The Reverend Dr. William Dodd was executed for the
capital offense of forgery, which Boswell called "the most
dangerous crime in a commercial country." The whole
episode is worth rereading, as is its sequel . . . in which,
less than a year after Dodd's execution, Johnson took occasion to pronounce that Dodd's sermons "were nothing,
sir." Presumably, Johnson felt that he had done his best
for Dodd and had no further obligation.

    [4] From article by George Stevens, editor and author. *Saturday Review.* 54:28-9.
S. 25, '71. Reprinted by permission.

In any event, there is no evidence that Johnson objected to the death penalty on principle or to its application in a case of forgery. The offense was removed from the list of capital crimes decades ago, leaving only murder and, in the United States, rape (in some states) as death-penalty offenses; kidnapping across state lines and skyjacking were to be added much later.

Now there is a movement, which promises to be successful, to abolish the death penalty altogether. [See "Death Penalty: A World Survey," in this Section, above.] This has been done in England. . . . What has happened to change public opinion so radically? Two centuries ago execution was a spectator sport; one century ago it aroused little opposition; now it may well be on the way to abolition. Why?

Well, quite a lot has happened, and there is danger in oversimplification; however, in my opinion, two causes dominate all the others. First, the law's delay. The case of Caryl Chessman, put to death in the gas chamber in California many years after his original conviction and following innumerable appeals, is an example of protracted legalisms that were bound, in time, to make the general public, or at least a substantial section of it, feel somehow responsible and even guilty. *We* had no right, it was felt, to take a life, whatever the guilt of the victim. There are similar cases: for instance, . . . [a] convict in New Jersey who has spent fourteen years on death row, longer than any other man in American history.

Now the Supreme Court is going to consider whether capital punishment is "cruel and unusual," and thus prohibited under the Constitution. "Cruel" has generally been taken to mean deliberate torture; "unusual" has referred to a penalty not generally applied to the same crime. But most Americans, like most Englishmen, have evidently come to understand that it is cruel to leave a person under sentence of death for a long period of uncertainty, and that it is undoubtedly unusual to put an individual to death, since it can happen to him only once. Also there is the lurking danger that the wrong person may be executed, and this is another of the leading causes of opposition to the death penalty. Sacco and Vanzetti [anarchists executed for murder in 1927] have not been forgotten.

On the other hand, many people have attempted to justify the death penalty for its supposed deterrent effect on others who, but for fear of a death sentence, might be tempted into the same crime. It is doubtful whether a consensus has been reached on this point. Indubitably, execution deters its victim from repeating his crime. This remark is not as frivolous as it may seem. How many "life" sentences dwindle to something like seven years? What justification the death penalty may have as a deterrent is in its preventing further murders, rapes, kidnappings, bombings, or whatever *by the same person*. Repetition of a crime by a released prisoner is by no means unheard of. The high incidence of recidivism is a statistical fact. Are potential victims not entitled to protection?

The foregoing points are familiar and need no development here. Hence, I come to the second reason why the death penalty is so widely and vigorously opposed. This reason involves a paradox, namely the growing acceptance of a certain concept: the sanctity of human life. Concurrent with this concept is a growing skepticism as to a future life. Our idea of the sanctity of human life used to depend upon our faith in the hereafter. . . . As long as people believed that the dead would be confronted by eternal judgment, it was easy to dictate the death sentence on earth. The judgment was going to follow sooner or later, and it might as well be sooner; at least it would be in the highest tribunal. Now, however, we—enough of us to make all the difference in this context—look upon death as extinction, and we recoil from the responsibility of extinguishing human life. Indeed, I think it is obvious that public opposition to the death penalty has increased in direct proportion to a diminishing belief in the hereafter.

The paradox repeats itself: Along with the decline of

belief in God, we have come to consider it God's privilege, not ours, to take human life. That is to say, human life identifiable in individual terms. We continue with only belated compunction to take human life—40,000 to 50,000 in the undeclared Vietnam war; more than 50,000 a year in automobile accidents; a hundred at a time in airplane disasters—and who, besides their families and friends, can name the victims? Even now [1971], when opposition to the Vietnam misadventure is overwhelming, a few of us still continue to speak of a "tolerable" number of casualties. We "tolerate" the victims of automobile accidents, however many are the result of corner-cutting in the automobile industry. We "tolerate" countless victims of the agricultural-industrial-political complex that depends on the sale of tobacco.

What it comes down to is that we are willing to put up with the extermination of human beings as long as we do not know who they are. But if a convicted criminal—a Chessman, a Sirhan Sirhan [convicted assassin of Senator Robert Kennedy]—manages to stay alive long enough after the death sentence to make an impression on the public *as an individual,* he arouses a sense of guilt in the public mind. This development usually leads to a clamor in the criminal's favor or at least to intensified pressure against the death penalty.

I am not taking sides on the issues; I leave that to the Supreme Court. What I am trying to convey is that if the life of a convicted murderer is worth saving, so much the more is that of a draftee sent to Southeast Asia; so much the more is the murderer's next victim. We are a long way from the ideal expressed by the late Dr. Albert Schweitzer in his phrase *reverence for life.*

II. CRIMINALS AND THE LAW

EDITOR'S INTRODUCTION

Several hundred people in the United States are currently on death row. Some have been there for years while the courts have reviewed the legal and constitutional aspects of their cases. Others are waiting while the constitutionality of the state law under which they were sentenced is tested in the light of the Supreme Court's 1976 rulings, including *Gregg v. Georgia*. Most, not surprisingly, would prefer to live, even if it means spending decades, or perhaps the rest of their lives, in prison.

The first article in this section examines the emotions and reactions of five different men under sentence of death. What is striking is the fact that sentences for the same crime differ so widely from place to place. Some people, convicted of a crime in which no life has been taken, are nevertheless sentenced to death. Others convicted of a crime in which a life has been taken receive life sentences, which means they will be eligible for parole at some time—some within a very few years.

The second article offers a view of recent activities of an anti-death-penalty organization, the Southern Coalition on Jails and Prisons, which is concerned with the ethical issues involved in killing a human being.

The next two selections deal with the Supreme Court's stand on the death penalty. The first of these excerpts examines the implications of the 1976 decision that the execution of a criminal does not necessarily constitute cruel and unusual punishment, which is prohibited by the Constitution of the United States. The second excerpt treats the Court decision in a more detailed manner, from the legal viewpoint.

The section concludes with a discussion of the death penalty in relation to the epidemic of politically oriented terrorism that has plagued almost every country in this decade. As the incidence of terrorist crimes has grown, more people and more governments (even those opposed to the death penalty) have called for the execution of those convicted of terroristic acts that cost the lives of chance victims. The situation is pointed up by the last article, which deals with the British and the Irish Republican Army.

FIVE UNDER SENTENCE
TO DIE SPEAK OUT [1]

Reprinted from *U.S. News & World Report.*

"Is It Fair They Get Life and Me Death?"

Charles Bryant says he favors capital punishment in some cases—but not for a crime such as his.

The crime that brought the twenty-three-year-old white steelworker to the death row of Angola [Louisiana] State Prison was "aggravated rape." He did not kill anybody. But because he used a gun in committing rape, he was ruled subject to Louisiana's new law that makes the death penalty mandatory in such cases.

Bryant describes such a law as "archaic and ignorant." He says: "Look at guys like Charles Manson—mass murderers—who'll be eligible for parole in seven years or so. Is it fair that they get life and me death?"

Bryant was twenty years old at the time he raped a young college girl in Monroe, Louisiana, in 1973. It was his first offense. Throughout the proceedings, Bryant was assured that the most he could get for his crime was life imprisonment. So it came as a shock to him when the judge announced that the death sentence was mandatory if the defendant was convicted as charged. The law making that sentence mandatory was passed to comply with a 1972 Supreme Court ruling. But the new law was nullified by the

[1] Article entitled "Death-Row Interviews" in *U.S. News & World Report.* 81:51-3. Jl. 12, '76.

Court in its July 2 [1976] decision. So Bryant escapes death.

As Bryant tells his story, it was a bad temper, a family quarrel—and some strange twists of fate—that brought him to death row. Traveling from Maryland, he had planned only a brief stop in Louisiana on his way to the West Coast. But one night he had a quarrel with his wife—who was killed in an auto accident shortly after his conviction in 1974.

The quarrel developed when Mrs. Bryant prodded him to see a doctor about blackouts he had been experiencing. "I didn't marry anyone to have them tell me what to do," Bryant retorted. "Well," said his wife, "if you want to kill yourself, why don't you just take a gun and get it over with?"

Out of spite, Bryant says, he grabbed a small pistol—a so-called Saturday-night special that he owned—and stormed out into the rainy night. "I shouldn't have gone out there," he says. "When I'm mad, I'm likely to do anything."

What he did was try to hitch a ride home to get out of the rain. Enraged that everyone passed him up, he finally stopped a car with two young girls in it.

"Move over," he told the girls. "I'm taking the wheel." After some talk and brandishing of his gun, Bryant admits, he had sexual relations with one of the girls. Did he actually rape her? "It's hard to figure," is his reply. "She said she didn't resist because I had a gun. Maybe that's right. I wouldn't want to make her out to be a tramp."

At Angola, Bryant is confined to a squalid, 6-by-8 cell twenty-three hours a day.

If given a choice between death and spending the rest of his life in this place, Bryant says he would choose death.

"I've got a daughter," he says, pointing to a picture of her that he wears on a chain around his neck. "She's three years old. And more than anything else, I'd like to get back to being a father. But even if they could fry me tomorrow, that would be preferable to spending the rest of my life here. This isn't living. It's just existing."

"I'd Support Death" for Some Crimes

Troy Leon Gregg does not deny that he shot and killed two men who gave him a ride as he was hitchhiking his way across Georgia in 1973, the day before Thanksgiving.

But Gregg does not think he should be executed for that. He claims he shot in self-defense when the two men attacked him. He says they had confided to him that they had committed a crime and were afraid he would tell on them.

Besides, Gregg says, he doesn't believe in execution for murder because: "People's been killing people since time began just to get ahead or stay alive in this world. It's sort of like in the forest. Wild animals."

However, Gregg believes that there are some crimes that warrant the death penalty. He says: "I would support the death penalty for child molesting—you know, out and out rape of a child, or an old person. I love old people and kids. Or for hijacking or treason, yes, I'd support the death penalty."

Even though he doesn't think he ought to die for the killings, they still prey on his mind. They caused him to have unpleasant dreams for a year afterward, and even now he occasionally has to take tranquillizers to sleep.

What hit him hardest, he says, was seeing the daughter of one of his victims "in court crying because her daddy was killed. That bothered me."

Another concern for Gregg was that his case might help to restore the death penalty—and the other inmates on Reidsville [Georgia] State Prison's death row would hold him personally responsible because his was one of the death sentences reviewed by the Court.

He said: "I really wouldn't want it on my conscience, knowing that my case helped bring the death penalty back."

As for his own fate, Gregg said: "I don't let it bother me. If a man lets it bother him he's gonna go crazy." But he couldn't help thinking: "If I had a life sentence, instead of a death penalty, I'd have some hope for the future while I'm still young, because in seven years I could come up for parole." Gregg, a white man, is twenty-eight years old.

Gregg's version of his killings is disputed by District Attorney Bryant Huff, who prosecuted his case in suburban Atlanta. Mr. Huff says Gregg killed the two men to steal their car and their money—about $400.

According to Huff, Gregg shot them as they stopped by the roadside to urinate, and then he walked to the ditch where the two had fallen and fired a bullet into the skull of each man. Says Mr. Huff:

"If anybody is ever deserving of the death penalty, Gregg would be."

A Murderer "Isn't Looking to Get Caught"

Jerry Lane Jurek says capital punishment does not deter crime. "If I was going to commit murder, I wouldn't be looking to get caught," says the twenty-five-year-old white man.

But Jurek was "caught," in the judgment of a jury that convicted him of killing a ten-year-old girl "while in the course of committing or attempting to commit kidnapping and/or forcible rape." He was sentenced to death.

Jurek remained confident to the very moment of the Supreme Court's decision that he would be spared from the electric chair. His confidence was based on his claim that he is innocent and did not get a fair trial.

Jurek's guilt or innocence was not an issue before the Court, however. The only issue in his appeal was whether the Texas law under which he was sentenced to death was constitutional.

He was arrested on August 17, 1973, for investigation into the disappearance the day before of Wendy Louise Adams, who was a daughter of a deputy sheriff in Cuero, Texas.

Authorities say he gave two confessions, admitting in both that he gave the Adams child a ride in his truck, took her to the nearby Guadalupe River, choked her and threw her body in the river. One statement contained an added admission that he raped her. There was no medical testimony at his trial to prove sexual assault.

With Jurek's aid, officials found the girl's body in the river. An autopsy disclosed that drowning was the cause of death.

In an interview on death row, Jurek denied the confessions and put the blame for the killing on a companion who was never arrested or charged.

Jurek's story is that he and the companion gave the girl a ride, their truck broke down near the river, and the friend escorted the girl to the river—but returned without her.

"When he told me he killed her, I thought he was just playing around," said Jurek.

The jury did not accept his story.

Jurek is a short, slight man, pale from more than two years on death row. He is low-keyed, talks little, rarely shows animation. His boyhood is one thing he discusses with great reluctance. He was the sixth of seven children in the family of a cotton mill worker in Cuero, a southeast Texas farm town of seven thousand.

After dropping out of school in the seventh grade, at age sixteen, he went to work as a laborer. His trouble with the law started early. At age fifteen, he was arrested and charged with raping a ten-year-old girl in Cuero. But the charges were dropped. Five years later, in Louisiana, he again was charged with rape, and again the charges were dropped. His record also includes a forgery charge on which he was never tried.

In 1971, Jurek married a sixteen-year-old girl. It was not a serene union. His wife wrote him a few days after his arrest and said she had given birth to a child. "She didn't say if it was a boy or a girl," said Jurek. He said he had not heard from his wife since then, and did not know where she was.

For Same Crime: Two Live, Two Get Death

Four men were involved in the same murder. Two were sentenced to death. The other two got off with thirty-five-year prison terms. That is why James Woodson thinks the North Carolina law on capital punishment is unfair and that he never should have been on death row.

Officials would not permit a *U.S. News & World Report* editor to interview Woodson. But, as pieced together from court records and talks with officials involved, his case is an unusual one.

Woodson was not even inside the E-Z Food Mart in Dunn, North Carolina, when the elderly woman who ran the store was shot to death and a bystander was wounded in a robbery on June 4, 1974. Woodson says he was just a lookout, sitting in the getaway car with the "wheelman," Johnnie Lee Carroll.

It was Luby Waxton who did the shooting, according to all accounts except Waxton's. Leonard Tucker was with Waxton and grabbed $280 from the store's till after the shootings.

All four could have been charged with a capital crime under North Carolina's felony-murder rule which makes a person guilty of murder—even though he personally did no killing—if a murder is committed by an accomplice in the commission of a felony.

But Tucker and Carroll made a deal with the prosecutor. In exchange for testifying against their two accomplices, Tucker and Carroll were permitted to plead guilty to armed robbery instead of murder. Thus they escaped the death penalty. Only Woodson and Waxton were sentenced to die.

It was seeming inequities such as this that civil-rights lawyers cited in arguing before the Supreme Court that capital punishment is inherently unfair because it is unequally applied. It was also argued that blacks are more likely to get the death penalty than whites for similar crimes. But in Woodson's case, all four of the men involved are black.

The Court, on July 2 [1976], voided the North Carolina law, nullifying the death sentences of Woodson and Waxton.

"It's How Much Justice You Can Buy"

Charles William Proffitt rejected an offer of a life sentence if he would plead guilty to a charge of stabbing a high-school wrestling coach to death while burglarizing the coach's home in Tampa, Florida, on July 10, 1973.

Proffitt rejected that offer. He says he would do the same thing again, because, he insists, he is innocent.

But a jury found the thirty-year-old white man guilty, and he was sentenced to die.

That grim fact hit him six months ago as, sitting in his 5-by-9 cell, he read a brief submitted in his case to the United States Supreme Court. He relates:

"I just couldn't believe that brief. I said, 'These people are going to kill me and there ain't a damn thing anybody's going to do about it.'

"On the evidence of the briefs that were submitted before the Supreme Court, I'd find me guilty, too, because there was nothing in my favor."

The Tampa coach was stabbed with a butcher knife when he stirred in his bed during a burglary. His wife was hit in the face when she awoke "to her husband's moans." She said she could not identify the killer.

The most damning evidence against Proffitt was testimony from a woman who shared a mobile home with the Proffitts. She said she heard Proffit in an ajoining bedroom confide the killing to his wife when he returned from a drinking bout in the early morning hours after the murder.

Proffitt denies that. He also claims the sketchy description of the killer given by the victim's wife did not match him. No fingerprints were found on the knife.

Although Proffitt has resigned himself to the prospect of his own execution, he is strongly opposed to the death penalty in general.

He contends that it is not a deterrent to crime and charges that it is applied in a discriminatory way.

Proffitt insists he wound up on death row because he couldn't afford to hire his own lawyer. He had a public defender. Of the way the death penalty is assessed, Proffitt says: "I think all reasonable thinking people will grant that it's not a just penalty that deals with everyone equally. It never has been. And it probably never will be, either. It's who you are, what you are, who you know, how much justice you can buy.

"If capital-punishment laws could be made just for everyone—which they can't be—then I would be in favor of it, seriously. But they do discriminate. All you have to do is look at the history of men on death row. You take anyone with a little bit of authority or money or who knows people—they're not on death row."

If execution were inevitable, Proffitt says: "Rather than sitting down in that electric chair, I'd rather go to a hospital somewhere and help somebody else—serve as a guinea pig to find a cure for cancer or something. I think a condemned man should be given a choice of whether he wanted to do that or not. If you're going to die, it's a more humane way of dying. And it would benefit society a hell of a lot more."

A Man "Can Straighten Up" If He Lives

Elmer Branch is alive today because the Supreme Court in 1972 held unconstitutional the Texas law under which he was sentenced to death. His sentence was commuted to life.

So Branch's fate was not at stake in the Court's latest decision [in 1976]. But he sees his case as an argument against the death penalty.

"I know I'm lucky," says Branch, a black man who was

one of twelve children in a rural family in Wilbarger County, Texas. "It has given me a chance to make it better for myself. I care for people now. I've really learned things that will help me rehabilitate myself. I've studied how other people behave, and I'm going to try to get to be the same way. I'm gonna stay out of trouble, no doubt about it."

Branch says he has a job waiting for him in Dallas. But prison officials say it could be a long wait.

Warden J. V. Anderson points out that Branch, "a fairly model prisoner" since leaving death row, is a second offender who once violated parole. Mr. Anderson will not predict what the parole board might do.

As might be expected, Branch is strongly opposed to capital punishment. "Any time someone commits a crime, there's something wrong with them," he says.

"If anybody has sense, he can straighten himself up in prison."

But, he adds, not if he's dead.

A CHRISTMAS VIGIL [2]

On Christmas Eve [1976], in front of . . . [North Carolina's] new legislative building, a small band of hardy and dedicated North Carolinians gathered in a candlelight vigil to protest the new death penalty law the 1977 legislature is expected to pass.

Bigger crowds gathered in front of the Duke University chapel in nearby Durham, and at Asheville, Charlotte and Greensboro. All across the South, in fact—at Memphis, Atlanta, Louisville, Dallas, New Orleans, Jackson, Birmingham, Tallahassee, Columbia and several other cities—candles were burning and hymns were being sung on Christmas Eve in public protest of the legal executions almost surely to take place next year.

[2] From article by Tom Wicker, staff correspondent, New York *Times.* p E9. D. 26, '76. © 1976 by The New York Times Company. Reprinted by permission.

Most of the vigils organized by the Southern Coalition on Jails and Prisons took place in front of courthouses, churches or state capitols. At Nashville the protesters gathered outside the state prison—where 41 persons are on Death Row at this Christmas season—in full view of many of the inmates.

The coalition, originally organized to further prison reform and improve the lot of inmates, turned its sights on the death penalty . . . [in 1976] after the Supreme Court ruled capital punishment constitutional under certain conditions; although the Court struck down death penalty laws in North and South Carolina and Louisiana, it upheld others in Georgia, Florida and Texas.

The South, of course, is prime territory for protesting the death penalty. Even after the Supreme Court rulings of . . . [1976] effectively reprieved the 122 persons on Death Row in North Carolina, the 47 in Louisiana and the 26 in South Carolina, 271 persons remain under sentence of death in the other Southern states—and that doesn't count the four persons in Virginia whose death sentences have been commuted by Governor Mills Godwin.

In Georgia, which has executed more people legally than any other state, 67 people are on Death Row and 10 of them—all males—have so nearly exhausted their rights of appeal as to be considered in immediate jeopardy of electrocution. They will go to their deaths, if they do, under a law signed by Governor Jimmy Carter, and now a model for new legislation in other states.

In Florida, where Attorney General Robert Shevin professes himself willing to "pull the switch" himself on the state's antiquated electric chair, seventy-seven men and one woman are under sentence of death. Six men are considered in immediate jeopardy, having exhausted all appeals except a final hearing and ruling by Governor Reubin Askew and the six cabinet members who make up the Executive Clemency Board. Mr. Askew and three other members of the board must concur if a death penalty is to be commuted.

Louisiana lost no time . . . in passing a new death penalty law after the Supreme Court ruled its previous statute unconstitutional. North Carolina, whose legislature meets only in odd years, is expected to pass a new law quickly, despite the determined opposition of the Southern Coalition. It's not clear how the laws of the other states might be viewed by the Supreme Court. . . .

In Mississippi, for example, twenty-five persons are on Death Row at Parchman Prison under a law similar to the Louisiana statute held invalid by the high court. These twenty-five—including five teen-agers, seventeen blacks, and four men with no previous convictions—cannot be sure, to this point, whether or not the death penalty hanging over their heads is constitutional.

Louisiana has some special problems. For one thing, its electric chair doesn't work anymore, not having been used since 1961—although it electrocuted 133 persons from 1930 to 1961—and the Texan the state used to hire to pull the switch, at $300 per execution, died several years ago.

The State Supreme Court, moreover, is insisting that the men and women reprieved when the old Louisiana death penalty law was struck down . . . [in 1976] be given the most severe alternative sentence available—life imprisonment for murder, for example. The reprieved persons and their lawyers are arguing that the legislature had provided no "alternative" to a mandatory death penalty—which is why the law was declared unconstitutional—and that therefore new trials must be held for all those reprieved in July.

In all the southern states, however, and as enthusiastic as legislators and the public may seem for death penalty laws, a strong undercurrent of opposition is flowing. The Southern Coalition on Jails and Prisons, with a chapter in every southern state, is a major instrument of that opposition. There may be some executions soon but they won't take place in the dark: as in its Christmas Eve vigils, the

coalition plans to keep right on raising what its director . . .
calls "the moral, religious and ethical issues involved in
killing any human being."

SPREADING IMPACT OF A HISTORIC
COURT DECISION [3]

Reprinted from *U.S. News & World Report*.

By upholding the constitutionality of capital punishment, the United States Supreme Court has opened the way
for a massive wave of executions.

Nearly 600 persons, including 12 women, are under death
sentences in 30 states. Their executions have been delayed,
awaiting the Supreme Court decision handed down on July
2 [1976]. Now, with legal doubts removed, many states can
proceed with executions. Most of them are prepared to do
so.

Although there has been no execution in this country
since 1967, . . . electric chairs and gas chambers have been
kept in readiness by most states with people on death row.
And many governors have said they will carry out the decision of the Supreme Court.

"Cruel, Unusual"?

The basic decision of the Court was that execution is
not "cruel and unusual punishment"—which is forbidden
by the Constitution. Said the opinion:

We hold that the death penalty is not a form of punishment
that may never be imposed, regardless of the circumstances of the
offense, regardless of the character of the offender, and regardless
of the procedure followed in reaching the decision.

The vote on this crucial issue was 7 to 2, with only the
Court's most consistently liberal Justices, William J. Brennan Jr., and Thurgood Marshall, dissenting.

By identical votes of 7 to 2, the Court specifically upheld the death-penalty laws of three states—Florida, Georgia

[3] From an article in *U.S. News & World Report*. 81:49-51. Jl. 12, '76.

and Texas. Those states have a combined total of 147 on death row who can now be executed unless errors are found in their trials or the governors commute their sentences.

However, the Supreme Court nullified the death-penalty laws of Louisiana and North Carolina, which have a combined total of 155 persons under sentence of death. Their sentences are now canceled, and probably will be commuted to prison terms.

The vote to strike down the North Carolina and Louisiana laws was 5 to 4.

Those laws, the majority held, do not conform to guidelines laid down by the Supreme Court in a 1972 decision.

That 1972 ruling struck down the death-penalty laws then in force, saying the application of the penalty was "arbitrary" and "capricious" because judges and juries had too much discretion in deciding who should be permitted to live and who should die.

After that ruling, thirty-five states wrote new death-penalty statutes in an attempt to meet the High Court's objections.

Florida, Texas and Georgia succeeded in that attempt, the Court held, but Louisiana and North Carolina did not.

In the death-penalty laws specifically upheld—those of Florida, Texas and Georgia—the Court found suitable standards to be followed by juries and judges in deciding who should be put to death and who should live. Those standards, the opinion said, "eliminated the arbitrariness and caprice" of the laws that were invalidated in 1972.

The Point: Objectivity

The key element that saved the three state laws upheld was that they make judges and juries consider both aggravating and mitigating circumstances about a crime before imposing any penalty of death. That, the Court said, makes the decisions objective, and thus acceptable.

The NAACP [National Association for the Advancement

of Colored People] Legal Defense and Educational Fund,
Inc., which closely follows cases involving the death penalty, found thirteen states with laws that are similar to
those upheld—and that presumably would pass High Court
muster. In those thirteen states are 144 persons under death
sentences, which now, apparently, can be carried out.

In upholding the death sentence as constitutional when
properly applied, the Court said:

The existence of capital punishment was accepted by the
Framers [of the Constitution]. For nearly two centuries this Court
has repeatedly recognized that capital punishment for the crime
of murder is not invalid per se—meaning "of itself."

Wide Acceptance

Also, the Court said, the fact that thirty-five states and
Congress have reenacted death-penalty laws since its 1972
ruling is a "marked indication of society's endorsement of
the death penalty for murder." And it added: "In a democratic society, legislatures—not courts—are constituted to re-
spond to the will and consequently the moral values of the
people."

As to the effectiveness of the death penalty, the Court
said: "There is no convincing empirical evidence either
supporting or refuting" the view that it deters murder. The
Court added: "The value of capital punishment as a deterrent of crime is a complex factual issue, the resolution of
which properly rests with the legislatures."

A check by *U.S. News & World Report* showed that several governors of states with large death-row populations
favor the death penalty and will proceed to carry it out.

Georgia Governor George Busbee co-authored his state's
capital-punishment law when he was a member of the legislature. Florida Governor Reubin Askew said: "I am convinced that the death penalty remains a deterrent under
certain circumstances, and should be retained for extreme
situations. I would sign an execution warrant."

Oklahoma Governor David Boren was quoted by his

official spokesman as being "personally in favor of the death penalty" and saying he "will let the law take its course." Texas Governor Dolph Briscoe also was quoted by his spokesman as favoring the death penalty.

"It's my personal belief the death penalty is a deterrent," said Governor Edwin W. Edwards of Louisiana, whose state's law was found invalid. . . .

Of eight states with large numbers of condemned inmates, six use the electric chair for executions. They are Arizona, Louisiana, Texas, Oklahoma, Georgia and Florida. California and North Carolina use gas chambers.

The Supreme Court limited its rulings to cases involving murder, since no other type of case was before it. The Court specifically left open the constitutionality of execution for rape, kidnapping, armed robbery or other crimes in which no human life is taken.

Although upholding the legality of capital punishment in general, the High Court—just as it did in 1972—laid down strict guidelines that states must follow in applying it.

In the Louisiana and North Carolina cases, five justices held that the states had gone too far in trying to remove the arbitrariness that the Court found objectionable in 1972. The new laws were found to be totally mandatory, allowing no consideration of aggravating or mitigating circumstances in a crime. And by doing that, the justices added, the two states had created a new legal problem.

Changing Standards

The court majority observed that the Eighth Amendment's "cruel and unusual punishment" clause draws much of its meaning from "the evolving standards of decency that mark the progress of a maturing society." And a totally mandatory death law was found not to comply with what the Court views those "evolving standards" to be today.

"One of the most significant developments in our society's treatment of capital punishment," the Court said, "has been the rejection of the common-law practice of in-

exorably imposing a death sentence upon every person convicted of a specified offense."

One Court objection to the North Carolina law was that
under it a jury is likely to acquit some factually guilty defendant in order to avoid triggering an automatic death
penalty. Juries, the Justices said, are not given proper guidelines on how to decide who should be spared and who
should not.

Also, the Court said, North Carolina's law is unconstitutional because of "its failure to allow the particularized
consideration of relevant aspects of the character and record
of each convicted defendant before the imposition upon
him of a sentence of death."

Less Severe, But—

Louisiana's law is less severe than North Carolina's in
that it has a more limited number of capital crimes. But
the court concluded: "The constitutional vice of mandatory
death-sentence statutes—lack of focus on the circumstances
of the particular offense and the character and propensities
of the offender—is not resolved by Louisiana's limitation of
first-degree murder to various categories of killings."

The Louisiana law was also found objectionable because
it gives juries an option of finding a defendant guilty of a
capital crime or a lesser offense without giving guidelines
to aid juries in making decisions. Thus, the Court said,
"there is an element of capriciousness in the Louisiana law"
that violates the 1972 ruling.

The NAACP Legal Defense Fund said sixteen states
have laws similar to those struck down in Louisiana and
North Carolina. Those states are now likely to rewrite their
laws or put them to a direct test in the Supreme Court,
with executions suspended until the validity of their laws
has been established.

In those sixteen states, there are now 145 persons under
death sentences—which are not likely to be carried out.

Justice Marshall, the Court's only black member, read

from the bench a stinging dissent to the majority ruling that upheld the death penalty.

Execution, he said, is an excessive penalty that neither deters crime nor is necessary to satisfy society's demands for retribution.

Justice Brennan, also dissenting, said: " 'Moral concepts' require us to hold that the law has progressed to the point where we should declare that the punishment of death, like punishments on the rack, the screw and the wheel, is no longer morally tolerable in our civilized society."

Justices Marshall and Brennan were so heavily outvoted, however, that this is now clear: Some states will have to revise their laws. A few may have trouble getting their new laws past the Supreme Court.

But the death penalty, in some form or other, is back—and likely to stay for many years to come.

NEW LIFE FOR THE DEATH PENALTY [4]

Four years ago [in 1972], when the Supreme Court announced its decision in *Furman v. Georgia,* opponents of the death penalty were cheered to find a majority on the Court willing to strike down death penalty statutes as unconstitutionally "cruel and unusual." Not only did this spare the lives of more than six hundred condemned persons; it also put the Court on record for the first time with a holding that the Constitution was not indifferent to the practice of capital punishment. True, the *Furman* decision did not strike down all possible forms of capital punishment legislation. It left untouched mandatory death penalty laws that leave the court no sentencing discretion for a person convicted of a capital crime; in 1972, a few such laws still remained in force around the country. The *Furman* ruling also indicated that discretionary death penalty laws with a two-stage trial, in which the court first settles the

[4] From an article by Hugo Adam Bedau, professor of philosophy at Tufts University. *Nation.* 223:144-8. Ag. 28, '76. Reprinted by permission.

issue of guilt and then in a second hearing consults a list of "aggravated" and "mitigating" circumstances to arrive at a sentence of death or of life, might not be unconstitutional. Nevertheless, the prevailing mood . . . in abolitionist circles occasionally verged on the euphoric.

However, encouraged by various spokesmen for the Nixon Administration, including the President himself, the national backlash against judicially imposed abolition was immediate. As of . . . [1976], thirty-five states had enacted new death penalty laws, more than five hundred persons were again under sentence of death, and the Supreme Court was weighing the constitutionality of these new statutes in cases on appeal from five states. The Solicitor General [of the United States], Robert H. Bork, . . . urged the Court to overturn its *Furman* ruling. He argued on several grounds, including a claim that the major factual assumptions under which the Court ruled against the death penalty had been shown, in the intervening four years, to be false. Public opinion, he said, now favored capital punishment; new evidence showed that executions were a deterrent to murder. . . . The NAACP [National Association for the Advancement of Colored People] Legal Defense Fund, counsel for most of the death penalty petitioners, asked the Court once and for all to strike down all death penalties, mandatory or discretionary, with or without statutory guidelines for sentencing. Their chief argument was that these differences in procedure were "cosmetic"; they only masked the arbitrary and discriminatory infliction of capital punishment. Probably neither side expected the Court to adopt such extreme solutions as overruling *Furman* or repudiation of all death penalties. But if the Court would not accept either of these extremes, how would it resolve the mixed legacy of *Furman?*

Gregg *and* Woodson *Rulings*

Speculation came to an abrupt end on July 2 [1976], when the Court announced its decision in five cases, of

which two—*Gregg v. Georgia* and *Woodson v. North Carolina*—will be much discussed. Certainly the most important was the Court's ruling in *Gregg v. Georgia*. By a majority of 7 to 2, the Court . . . said that "the punishment of death does not invariably violate the Constitution." Writing for the Court in a plurality opinion joined by Justices Powell and Stevens, Justice Potter Stewart argued that the Court cannot compel a legislature "to select the least severe penalty" appropriate to grave crimes. Nor can it be maintained, Stewart insisted, that "death is disproportional in relation to the crime" of murder. "It is an extreme sanction, suitable to the most extreme of crimes." Therefore, since life imprisonment is not required by the Constitution as the punishment suitable for the gravest of crimes, and since death is not prohibited, the punishment of death is permissible, provided the sentencing jury in a capital case has its discretion "suitably directed and limited so as to minimize the risk of wholly arbitrary and capricious action." After scrutiny of the post-*Furman* Georgia death penalty statute for murder under which Gregg was convicted and sentenced, the Court concluded that it insured the required "direction" and "limitations" and thus was not unconstitutional.

The distinctive features of the Georgia law on which the Supreme Court rested its favorable judgment were several: a two-stage capital trial, the second part of which was devoted solely to the issue of sentencing; statutory provision for the jury to consider aggravating and mitigating circumstances in order to channel its assessment of facts pertinent to its choice of punishment; a written ("special") verdict by the court as to its findings relevant to the sentence it imposed; automatic review by the state Supreme Court of both the legal and factual issues decided by the jury as they relate to sentencing.

In two of the other death penalty cases decided the same day, *Proffitt v. Florida*, and *Jurek v. Texas*, death penalty statutes for murder in Florida and Texas were upheld on the strength of the holding in *Gregg*. The fact that the

Florida and Texas procedures differed considerably from those of Georgia's did not perturb the majority of the Court. The similarities in "directing" and "limiting" the jury's discretion, the Court majority implied, were more important than the differences.

In a footnote to his *Gregg* opinion, Justice Stewart noted that the constitutionality of the Georgia death penalty statutes for murder is not to be taken as implying that the death penalty for a crime that "does not result in the death of any human being—such as rape, burglary and armed robbery" is also constitutional. . . .

In its decisions in the other two death penalty cases, the Court moved in a direction somewhat at odds with its rulings in *Gregg, Proffitt* and *Jurek*. In *Woodson v. North Carolina,* the Court declared that the mandatory death penalty for first-degree murder enacted by the North Carolina legislature in 1974 was unconstitutionally cruel and unusual. Again in a plurality opinion for the Court, Justice Stewart argued that in this day and age mandatory death penalties fly in the face of the "evolving standards of decency" the Court has long acknowledged as central to the determination of what is "cruel and unusual punishment." During the previous century, mandatory death penalties were rejected as "unduly harsh and unworkably rigid" in favor of discretionary sentencing. Thus, their current reintroduction constitutes an unworkable throwback to the past.

The trouble with such penalties, argued Stewart, is that they treat all persons convicted of a given offense "not as uniquely individual human beings, but as members of a faceless, undifferentiated mass to be subjected to the blind infliction of the penalty of death." Instead, what is needed—consistent with the requirements imposed four years ago in *Furman*—are "objective standards to guide, regularize, and make rationally reviewable the process for imposing a sentence of death."

In the last of its death penalty cases, *Roberts v. Louisiana,* the Court invoked its ruling in *Woodson* to set aside as unconstitutionally cruel and unusual Louisiana's mandatory death penalty for murder. Thus, thanks to the rulings in *Woodson* and *Roberts,* at least 170 condemned persons in these two states will have their death sentences voided and in the months ahead they will be returned to lower courts for resentencing to imprisonment.

There is only one explicit qualification to the Court's condemnation of mandatory death penalties in *Woodson* and *Roberts.* The Court noted that the constitutionality of mandatory death penalties for life-term prisoners convicted of murder or aggravated assault had not been presented in the cases on appeal and therefore was not settled by the *Woodson* ruling. It is worth noting that Jimmy Carter said in a . . . press interview that, although he now was generally opposed to the death penalty, the one exception he still would favor was for "lifers" who commit a second murder while in prison.

Effect of Gregg *and* Woodson

The chief effect of the rulings in the two leading cases, *Gregg* and *Woodson,* is that the Supreme Court has reaffirmed and clarified its *Furman* ruling, thereby meeting the most persistent demand of its critics during the last four years. The plurality opinion in *Gregg* by Justices Stewart, Powell and Stevens emphasized that the *Furman* decision is valid constitutional law. This effectively lays to rest any possibility that the Burger Court will overturn the *Furman* ruling. In the gloom spread by the *Gregg* decision, it is important not to lose sight of this solid confirmation of *Furman.* On the other hand, of the two possibilities left open by *Furman*—mandatory and "guided discretion" statutes— only the latter now remains. The states, as well as Congress, now have much clearer guidance as to the sort of capital statutes they can constitutionally enact. The puzzle set by the *Furman* Court has now been solved by the *Gregg* Court. The national posture on the death penalty, so far as its "cruelty and unusualness" is concerned, is stabilized. Dur-

ing the next year or so, one can expect, several legislatures
will enact statutes patterned after those upheld in Georgia,
Florida and Texas.

What other effects are the *Gregg* and *Woodson* rulings
likely to have? It now seems improbable that the Supreme
Court will again in this century rule forcefully and directly
against capital punishment on any constitutional ground.
During the past decade, the strongest untested argument
available to abolitionists—that the death penalty is per se
"cruel and unusual punishment," no matter for what crime
and no matter how administered—has been rejected by a
large majority of the Court. Only two justices, Brennan
and Marshall, have embraced the abolitionists' preferred
interpretation of the Eighth Amendment. Both Stewart and
White, who were part of the slender five-man majority in
Furman . . . [in 1972], backed off from the unconstitutional
per se interpretation sought by the [NAACP] Legal Defense
Fund in *Gregg*. Justice White even refused to join Stewart
in the *Woodson* majority to condemn mandatory death
sentences. (Justices Powell and Stevens, with Stewart, Brennan and Marshall, constituted the 5 to 4 majority in *Woodson* and *Roberts*.) With such a substantial portion of the
Court thus turning its back on judicial abolition by the
federal courts, it is unlikely that newer and probably weaker
constitutional arguments will prevail where the stronger
and more familiar ones have failed.

Fate of Death-Row Prisoners

Uppermost in many minds is the fate of the 150 or so
death-row prisoners in Georgia, Texas and Florida. What
lies ahead for them? Are they likely to face the execution
chamber—unused anywhere in the United States since
June 1967 in Colorado—and if so, how soon? . . . The *Gregg*
ruling, addressed solely to the issue of sentencing, leaves untouched and undecided any issues affecting the conviction
in each of these cases. Pending the resolution of the constitutionality of the death sentence itself, none of the sub-

stantive issues surrounding the convictions in these 150 cases has been litigated. In many instances, lawyers are confident, reversals will be obtained in state or federal courts.

Unlikely though it might seem, the *Gregg* ruling may have some hidden advantages for defense lawyers with capital cases. By insisting that the trial courts and state appellate courts scrutinize carefully the characteristics of a convicted murderer prior to issuing a death sentence, it becomes possible to litigate issues hitherto not easily presented to courts. Since many of the Georgia, Florida and Texas death sentences were imposed after only the most perfunctory appraisal of mitigating circumstances, a virgin field of argument is now opened up for defense lawyers to explore in future cases. Thus, although *Gregg* thoroughly squelched some abolitionist hopes, it opened up new possibilities that with imaginative and resourceful litigation may avoid or nullify many death sentences.

How will *Gregg* and *Woodson* affect the death penalty in other states? Aside from steering legislatures toward guided discretion statutes and the two-stage trial in capital cases, the *Gregg* ruling probably will be applied directly to uphold capital statutes in several other states. The Arkansas, Arizona, Colorado and Ohio death statutes seem fundamentally like those upheld in Georgia, Florida and Texas. Thus, another seventy or so death-row prisoners are likely to lose their appeals to the Supreme Court for the same reason that Gregg lost his. Perhaps . . . this may culminate in pressures on several governors to commute death sentences wholesale.

One of the galling features of the *Gregg, Profitt* and *Jurek* decisions is the way the Court reacted, or rather failed to react, to the social science research published in the years since *Furman*. With perhaps one exception, the Court passed it by without significant acknowledgment, discussion or rebuttal. This was especially conspicuous in the *Gregg* ruling. Both in the written briefs and in the oral

argument, Legal Defense Fund attorneys had labored to
show that such evidence as was available to qualified observers pointed unmistakably to the conclusion that the
post-*Furman* death statutes achieved little or no change
from the pre-*Furman* statutes, with their unbridled discretion and arbitrary and discriminatory impact. Justice Stewart's opinion in *Gregg* magisterially ignored this evidence,
even as it rejected the contention in question.

Similarly, the Court indicated that it was impressed by
public opinion surveys (which in recent years report that
the American public favors the death penalty by a margin
of roughly 2 to 1), despite the superficiality of these findings as shown by critical social scientists. Only Justice Marshall, in dissent, noted that public opinion is relevant to
interpreting the Constitution only when it is "informed"
opinion. On the deterrence question, the *Gregg* Court did
pause to note that, despite a heated debate for the past few
years, the empirical evidence is "simply . . . inconclusive."
Nevertheless the Court immediately added (without a scin-
tilla of evidence cited in support) that "the death penalty
undoubtedly is a significant deterrent" in some cases: murder for hire and murder by a life-term prisoner. For social
scientists and jurists who had expected that this round of
death penalty cases would find the Supreme Court resting
its decision, at least in part, on the results of careful and
relevant empirical investigations, the *Gregg* decision can
be viewed only as a bitter disappointment. . . . [In 1972],
in his dissent in *Furman,* Chief Justice Burger complained
of the "paucity" of evidence relied on by the majority ruling in favor of abolition. . . . [The 1976] ruling in *Gregg*
rests on even less.

Retributive Justice

However, it is not so much from a scientific as from a
moral point of view that the rulings in *Gregg, Proffitt* and
Jurek are unconvincing. It is troubling to see the majority
in *Gregg* invoke the constitutional legitimacy of retribution

in punishment, and of the death penalty as an instrument of just retribution. The Court seems to overlook the fundamental fact that punishment, by its very nature, is retributive. This is so because punishments are designed to pay back to offenders suffering and indignities akin to those the offender unjustly imposed on the innocent victim. Hence, imprisonment for murder, no less than the death penalty, is retributive. The question, of course, is whether it is retributive enough. The *Gregg* Court writes as if individuating a death sentence for a particular offender, a trial court serves the retributively just purpose, under the Constitution, of making the most severe sentence fit the gravest criminal homicides.

But this line of reasoning is open to the Court only if it is also ready to argue that retributive justice, under the Constitution, is not met when all murderers are sentenced only to imprisonment, as they will be in a state which has abolished (or failed to reenact) the death penalty. The Court, of course, has no intention of advancing any such objection. The result is a dilemma. If, as the *Gregg* Court insists, the Constitution permits the death penalty because of its retributive superiority to lesser punishments for murder, then it is difficult to see why the Court extends constitutional toleration, as it does, to less severe . . . punishments for this crime. On the other hand, if, as the Court implies, any punishment other than death decreed by a legislature and imposed by a trial court is adequately retributive, it is hard to see how retribution can be trotted out to bolster the added severities unique to the death penalty. The principles of retributive justice simply are not a legitimate basis for construing the constitutional prohibition against "cruel and unusual punishment" in a manner tolerant of the death penalty.

Hidden beneath the veneer of constitutional argument is the plain evidence that the Court has proved itself arbitrary and discriminatory in its defense of the death penalty. Where the *Woodson* decision will eventually free scores of prisoners from execution, the *Gregg* decision may consign hundreds to their deaths.

Where is the rational difference in the crimes and criminals that justifies this line drawn by the Court, upholding death sentences in Georgia but condemning the same sentences across the state line in North Carolina? Why should Gregg, a hitchhiker convicted of robbing and murdering the men who gave him a ride, have his death sentence upheld, when Woodson, convicted of robbing and killing a storekeeper, has his death sentence overturned? Why shouldn't both, or neither, be spared? It is more than ironic that if Woodson had robbed and killed in Georgia, and Gregg in North Carolina, it would be Gregg, not Woodson who was spared and Woodson, not Gregg whose death sentence was sustained. Is this even-handed, rational justice where life and death are at issue?

If, as the Court said in *Woodson,* the death penalty is "qualitatively different" from imprisonment, it is odd that the difference seems to arouse the disapproval of the Court only when it occurs in conjunction with death statutes of mandatory or unlimited discretionary application. Nowhere in its recent decisions does the Court address this issue, and no plausible answer is to be found. No doubt unintentionally, the Court's decisions . . . are the perfect proof of the major contention urged by abolitionists during the past decade. In this country, today, it is simply not possible to have a death penalty applied with uniform, predictable, rational impact all across the land. Instead, we can have capital punishment only if it is unpredictable, arbitrary and infrequent in its application. Retributive justice of this sort is simply not justice at all, because it is inequitable.

Of course, the unconstitutionality of capital punishment has never been the major objection. Until fifteen years ago, save for a few mavericks, no one gave any credence to the possibility of ending the death penalty by judicial interpretation of constitutional law. Legislative repeal and executive commutation of sentence were always the chief focus of abolitionist efforts, despite the discouraging results year after year. Thus, the news of Canada's abolition of capital punishment [in 1976] in a close parliamentary vote is a sharp reminder that our national posture on this subject is increasingly at variance with that of our traditional neighbors and allies, and that such progress toward total abolition as we have achieved in recent years has been secured not by executive or legislative leadership but by the judiciary. As in most legislative policies affecting civil liberties and civil rights, there are limits to what even the most enlightened appellate courts can do when left adrift by the other branches of government. On the matter of capital punishment, those limits may have been reached, at least for the moment, in *Gregg* and *Woodson.*

It is difficult to believe that the nine justices of the Supreme Court can contemplate their decisions in *Gregg, Proffitt* and *Jurek* with any real satisfaction. They have put aside their personal scruples against the death penalty in the name of federalism, judicial restraint, legislative deference and retribution. Thus, two days before the nation's Bicentennial, the world is told that, so far as the federal Constitution is concerned, our "natural rights to life, liberty and the pursuit of happiness" yield not a condemnation of, but a permission to, death-inclined legislatures and courts—at least where the punishment of murder is concerned. Some will find this, as I do, disheartening. We had hoped the Court might see the Constitution differently in our time, and say so in accents that would command agreement and respect.

TERRORISM AND THE DEATH PENALTY [5]

A spate of terrorist activity in the past several months has focused public attention on terrorism more than at any

[5] Article by Thomas Perry Thornton, member of the policy planning staff of the United States Department of State. *America.* 135:410-12. D. 11, '76. Reprinted with permission of *America.* All rights reserved. © 1976 by America Press, 106 W. 56th St., New York, NY 10019.

time since the Munich massacre of Israeli Olympic ath-
letes . . . [in 1972]. The most dramatic of these recent acts
were the hijackings of an American aircraft by Croatians
[September 1976] and of a French plane by Palestinians
[June 1976]. The latter caught particular public attention
because of the dramatic rescue operation mounted at Entebbe while the plane was under the eye of Ugandan dic-
tator Idi Amin.

Hijackings and other forms of hostage-taking are the
terrorist act par excellence of our time, just as the bombing
of crowned heads was at the turn of the century. The Air
France hijacking, for instance, attracted much more attention here than did the murder by terrorists of two American diplomats in Beirut, even though there were no American lives lost at Entebbe. The reason is simple: hijackings
not only affect a broad range of people with whom the
public can readily identify; they are also protracted affairs
that get extensive play in the media. A murder is top news
for one day while a hijacking can go on for as long as a
week.

There are, of course, many forms of terrorism other
than hijacking and hostage-taking, such as bombing, assassination and armed robbery. Whatever the form, however,
terrorist acts share a crucial characteristic. They have a high
symbolic content in that they seek to make an impact on
public opinion—to gain support if possible, but at least to
draw attention to the terrorists' causes. Some instances, such
as the Croatian hijacking, are pure public relations ven-
tures, but even those that have a more specific goal are
usually successful in engaging the public consciousness.

Once engaged, however, public opinion sets forth its
own demands. It views terrorism not simply as another kind
of ordinary crime, but as an especially outrageous form of
behavior that demands exemplary punishment. The spectacular rescue at Entebbe had a high emotional appeal precisely because it was gratifying at the symbolic level. The
drama of the rescue exceeded that of the hijacking itself so

that justice was seen to be done in a satisfying way. The punishment fit the crime.

Deus ex machina outcomes of the Entebbe variety are not common, however, and few terrorist episodes have results that satisfy the public. Terrorists mostly go scot-free for one reason or another, and when they are captured, trials tend to drag on. Even the ultimate sentence of imprisonment does not seem to match the gravity or the emotional impact of the offense. Rather, major successes over the past years in dealing with terrorism have been in the unglamorous areas of prevention carried out by police and intelligence forces that operate far from public view. In fact, we have greatly reduced the incidence of terrorism that we otherwise might have expected, but it is the dramatic terrorist successes that capture public attention and shape the public response to this challenge to international order. It is hardly surprising, then, that demands for action against terrorism focus on symbolically satisfying and dramatic means of prevention and retribution. Even less surprisingly, the proposals made for prevention and retribution are often bizarre and of questionable efficacy and legality. The death penalty appears high on most people's lists, and the problem of hostage-taking is at the center of concern.

A soberly argued discussion of ways and means of coping with terrorism was offered by C. L. Sulzberger in his New York *Times* column of July 7, just after the Entebbe operation. Mr. Sulzberger focused on practical steps rather than symbolic retribution, concluding his piece with a plea for executing "condemned" terrorists. Although he did not spell this idea out in detail and the idea is not novel, his article makes a good point of departure for discussing terrorism and the death penalty, because it raises the matter rationally and because Mr. Sulzberger is otherwise opposed to capital punishment.

The argumentation for executing terrorists runs as follows: when a person is apprehended and imprisoned for any kind of terrorist act, there is a substantial likelihood that other like-minded terrorists will seek to force his release by taking hostages and threatening to kill them unless their imprisoned comrade is set free. The nation holding the terrorist prisoner faces a dilemma: either acquiesce in the demand and release the prisoner, thus demonstrating once again that terrorism is a low-risk undertaking even for those who are caught; or refuse to yield to the demand and thereby endanger the lives of the innocent hostages. Indeed, even if the demands are met, the hostages will still have been subjected to the very considerable dangers routinely involved in such a situation. In Mr. Sulzberger's words, "every live convicted terrorist in prison increases the chance of dead innocents abroad."

If, however, convicted terrorists are executed, there will be no reason for their comrades to take hostages to force their release. At most there might be attempts to exact revenge. These, however, would probably be directed at police or judicial officials rather than innocent people who had no connection with the terrorist's execution and with whom the public does not readily identify.

Terrorism is, in fact, along with treason and murder committed by prisoners serving life terms, one of the prime tests of arguments against the death penalty. Terrorism is outrageous in the public view. The line of argumentation set forth by Mr. Sulzberger and others has a compelling rational content. But the death penalty is a gravely serious measure to invoke in any circumstance, and in this case there are weighty legal and logical counterarguments in addition to the unavoidable moral considerations that weigh against any taking of life.

The initial problem is that of definition. What is, after all, *terrorism?* Its definition has been debated extensively in the scholarly literature for years. I am well satisfied with one I offered over a decade ago—"a symbolic act designed to influence political behavior by extranormal means, entailing the use or threat of violence"—but I have no illusions that this definition or any other could or should stand up before a court of law. Although we can define the phenomenon of terrorism broadly and certain acts are clearly terrorist by any reasonable definition, there are immense gray areas that would open the way to serious miscarriages of justice, for *terrorism* is a highly subjective concept. Attempts to develop international law concerning terrorism have foundered on the fact that one man's terrorist is the other man's freedom-fighter, whether he be a member of [Palestinian] Black September or the [Jewish] Stern Gang [active before the establishment of the state of Israel].

This semantic ambiguity was illustrated during Daniel Patrick Moynihan's successful bid for the Democratic Senate nomination in New York . . . [in 1976]. The former UN Ambassador suggested that his antiterrorist record in the UN would in some way be relevant to stopping "terror" in the darkened streets of New York City, but in fact it is hard to see any connection between muggings and aircraft hijackings. In the present political and social context, we must live with the fact that "terrorism" is simply not a useful way of categorizing antisocial behavior, let alone a legally tenable definition of a capital crime.

The definitional problem cannot be avoided by defining hostage-taking, rather than terrorism, as the crime that triggers the death penalty. First, this would do little to meet the requirement of making terrorists harmless, since not all terrorist acts involve taking hostages or hijacking. (Very little IRA [Irish Republican Army] activity, for example, has involved hostage-taking.) Second, there are no doubt hundreds of hostage incidents in the United States every year, few of which have anything to do with terrorism and many of which are not very serious. Do we really want to extend the death penalty to all of these?

In a sense, terrorism is a description of a state of mind rather than a definition of specific criminal acts. A man may commit a political murder that can be defined reasonably as terrorism, and under many legal systems he would receive a death sentence. But a "terrorist" may also commit armed robbery that does not result in any deaths, and he would not be likely to receive more than a prison term. If, however, we define terrorism as the crime, irrespective of the content of the terrorist act, then both men would be executed in order to prevent like-minded comrades from seizing hostages to free either of them. In doing this, we would have moved onto novel legal terrain: we would be executing people, not for specific crimes that they have committed, but for what other people might do on their behalf. As illustrations of the logical dilemma let us take two hypothetical cases.

The first would be the semi-active accomplice of a fatal hijacking operation who provided shelter for the terrorist hijackers before the operation took place. Even if conspiracy to murder could be proved, the death penalty would be an extremely harsh sentence to impose. Yet this accomplice, if jailed, would be just as likely to trigger a subsequent hostage-taking operation to force his release as would terrorists who committed more serious crimes. The purpose of such operations is to generate publicity and get people out of jail. The specific grounds of imprisonment is a secondary consideration.

Closer to home, there is the Patricia Hearst case. Let us assume she had been captured during the bank robbery she participated in. Bank robbery is not a capital crime, but had there been legislation on the books in California that prescribed death for terrorists, Miss Hearst would certainly have had to be executed. The Symbionese Liberation Army was, if nothing else, a terrorist organization, and prevailing opinion at the time would have held that her SLA colleagues would likely have sought to force her release from prison by taking hostages. But would justice have been served?

A final dilemma is offered in two hypothetical hijacking

cases. In one, an embezzler hijacks a plane and holds the passengers hostage in order to escape from the law. In the other, terrorists hold passengers hostage in pursuit of some political goal. Both fail and are captured, and the operations are bloodless. Hijacking that does not result in death is no capital crime under US law, but the terrorists would be executed on the grounds that their sympathizers might try to force their release. The embezzler received only an additional jail term, because there is no reason to believe that anybody would mount a rescue operation on his behalf. Yet both have equally endangered lives by taking hostages. This would be a grossly unequal application of the law and would no doubt be unconstitutional in the United States.

We encounter still a further problem. In law-governed societies, at least, capital trials tend to take a considerable amount of time, and review and appeal processes can drag on even longer before a death sentence is carried out. Thus, would-be rescuers of captured terrorists still could have ample time to mount their rescue operation. Indeed, the chances of their doing so could be greatly increased if their imprisoned comrades face execution, for under present circumstances the only pressing motive to force a release is a political one. Making terrorism a capital crime could in this way raise the likelihood of hostage-taking operations, quite the opposite of what was originally intended. There is an obvious logical remedy: instruct law-enforcement officers to kill terrorists promptly upon capture, acting as apprehender, judge and executioner. The grotesqueness of this "logical conclusion" should be painfully obvious to all but the most hardened viewers of late-night Westerns.

Finally, although deterrence is not the issue at stake in this matter, it must be noted that there seems to be no correlation between deterrence and the death penalty. The threat of capital punishment is particularly unlikely to deter terrorists, given their total commitment to fighting a political or social order that they find abhorrent.

We cannot really divorce the question of capital punishment for terrorists from the broader question of the morality of the death penalty, as I have done thus far. It was a fitting coincidence that the Entebbe raid came within a few days of the Supreme Court's decision on *Gregg v. Georgia* that reopened the possibility of the death penalty in the United States, including, presumably, for terrorism if we choose to take that path. This is not the place to argue the pros and cons of the death penalty in general, but there is something to be learned by looking at the matter in the light of the terrorist problem.

If abhorrence of the perceived injustice of the political and social order is what drives men to terrorism and contempt for human life, the terrorist is only the child of his age. The criterion for capital punishment set forth in *Gregg v. Georgia* ("an expression of society's moral outrage at particularly offensive conduct") is simply the mirror image of the terrorist's outlook. It, too, decides that the price of outrage at this time in history is fairly set at human life. We must recognize that *Gregg v. Georgia* is not an arbitrary plunge backward in mankind's progress toward civilization and humaneness, decided in isolation by five misguided men. Rather, it is an accurate reflection of the attitudes of much of American society—a point that Justice Potter Stewart made abundantly clear in his decision. Many, perhaps most, Americans find the death penalty neither cruel nor unusual as an expression of their outrage. Taken together with widespread attitudes favoring liberal abortion laws, it is evident that a disturbingly large number of Americans do not place all that high a value on human life—at least not on the lives of inconvenient members of society. Terrorists, whether of the Black September or Hitler type, only take this attitude to its logical conclusion. Many of them are at least fully consistent in showing contempt for their own lives as well.

If this is the case, then the legal, moral and logical arguments about executing terrorists may not be relevant. Perhaps society does demand exemplary and symbolically satisfying retribution against terrorists as well as murderers—and, ultimately, rapists and muggers and others who commit "outrageous" crimes. After *Gregg v. Georgia,* the gates are open.

Increasingly throughout the civilized world, there is a widespread view that capital punishment is incompatible with humane society, and this growing consensus is one of the more substantial ethical accomplishments of recent years. [See "Death Penalty: A World Survey" in Section I, above.] Despite the court ruling, we still have hope to save it in the United States. There would be a spectacular irony, however, if terrorism were among the crimes that urge our society to restore the death penalty. The ultimate aim of the true terrorist is to undermine the values of the society that he detests. Mr. Sulzberger's abandonment of a long-held moral opposition to capital punishment shows that in one case, at least, the terrorists have been successful. Both individuals and societies at times take on the attributes of their tormentors as a means of self-protection. If we abandon our respect for life in order to cope with the terrorist, we will become an unwitting but sadly willing accomplice in his attempt to destroy us.

Stalin and Hitler, as well as contemporary dictators, have shown us that ruthless repression can root out the terrorism of political agitation. The price, however, has been the institution of another kind of terror. If twentieth century history has taught us anything, it is that the terrorism of governments is vastly more destructive, both physically and morally, than the actions of a few dozen, or even hundreds of bomb-throwers, hijackers and assassins. Terrorism is real, and it is gruesome. It does not, however, pose the "clear and present danger" that, in the words of a much better Supreme Court opinion, is the sole justification for a society's violating its own values in the cause of self-preservation.

THE BRITISH AND THE IRA [6]

To the great credit of the British Parliament and to the relief of most British Christians, the House of Commons has rejected, by a vote of 361 to 232, a proposal that would have reintroduced capital punishment into the British legal system, albeit confining execution to terrorists found guilty of murder.

The pressure on members of Parliament was considerable. During the past eighteen months terrorists of the Irish Republican Army have extended their activities from Northern Ireland to a number of British cities. While one cannot say that the streets of London are no longer safe for the ordinary citizen, certainly the chances of meeting a violent death are much higher than at any time since the end of World War II. Car owners may find an explosive device attached to the underside of their parked vehicle, and those who frequent the more expensive restaurants in London's West End may have their meal interrupted by a bomb tossed into the doorway from a passing car.

Just fourteen days before the debate in Parliament, London experienced its first terrorist assassination [November 27, 1975]. Early in November, Ross McWhirter—editor and publisher of the *Guinness Book of World Records* and well known in Britain as an espouser of right-wing causes—launched an appeal for £50,000 to provide rewards for information leading to the arrest of terrorist bombers. His own reward for this enterprise was a bullet in the head and another in the chest from two gunmen who confronted him one evening in the garden of his North London home.

The Debate in Parliament

Assassinations of this kind are commonplace in Northern Ireland where, unfortunately, they tend to be taken for

[6] Article, datelined London, by Trevor Beeson, European correspondent for *The Christian Century*. *Christian Century*. 93:60-2. Ja. 28, '76. Copyright 1976 Christian Century Foundation. Reprinted by permission.

granted, but the possibility that well-known public figures
may be killed in the streets of London or in their own
homes has aroused a good deal of anger in England. The
latest Gallup poll shows 88 percent of the population in
favor of executing terrorists.

Leading churchmen have, however, taken a different
view. In a letter to the *Times*, the archbishops of Canter-
bury and York and the leaders of other non–Roman Catholic churches stated their firm opposition to the reintroduction of capital punishment for any offense:

> For the State to bring back execution, and so return to a relic
> of a bygone age, would be to concede that Britain feels itself
> forced to resort to methods of law-enforcement commonly used
> in a political context by nations whose methods we properly con-
> demn as tyrannical. . . . Our will to build a compassionate society
> leads us to the conviction that justice is not best served by retri-
> bution. The sanctity of human life is indivisible.

The debate in Parliament was not, however, concerned
primarily with the moral issue but rather with the most
effective way of halting terrorism. Some who strongly oppose capital punishment for ordinary murder believe that
terrorists are a special case. Bombers are, it is argued, engaged in warfare; they should therefore be treated like
other armed enemies of the state. Moreover, life sentences
are no deterrent since terrorists anticipate amnesties as
part of a future political deal.

Home Secretary Roy Jenkins had practical reasons for
rejecting this argument. He said that the creation of martyrs
would serve only to inflame the violent elements in the
Irish community, and he had no doubt that if any terrorists
were executed their colleagues would mark the occasion
with even more widespread bombings. It would, he insisted,
be impossible to distinguish between those who actually
committed acts of terrorism and those who provided them
with weapons or afforded them shelter. Members of juries
and others involved in the trials of terrorists would be put
at risk, and the work of the people would be made even

more difficult—a view shared by all the senior police officers.
Jenkins preferred to concentrate on improving security and
warned terrorists that under no circumstances would those
sentenced to life imprisonment ever be amnestied. This em-
phasis on the importance of adequate security was strikingly
vindicated a few days later when the London police arrested
four leading IRA terrorists at the end of a dramatic siege
in which a middle-aged couple were held hostage in their
own home.

Important Questions Underscored

The decision not to reintroduce capital punishment for
terrorists has, however, underscored two important questions. The first of these involves the relationship between
Parliament and the electorate. If 88 percent of the population believes that bombers should be executed, shouldn't
these voters' representatives in Parliament treat their viewpoint more seriously and pass the necessary legislation?
What does democracy involve in these circumstances?

One answer is that politicians are obliged to act in what
they conceive to be the best interests of their constituents,
though this may involve going against the expressed wishes
of those who voted them into office. This is a tricky position
to occupy, since a degree of paternalism or elitism is implied, but under the British system it is certainly desirable
that members of Parliament follow their own consciences
rather than simply express the views of those who, however
understandably, seek uncomplicated answers to complex
questions.

The second question concerns the ultimate solution of
the Irish problem—which now seems as elusive as ever, with
the British government doing no more than pursuing a
"holding" policy in the hope that with the passage of time
the various factions in Northern Ireland will come to recognize the futility of violence and cease to support the terrorists, who constitute only a tiny minority of the population. Thus isolated, the terrorists will be defeated by the

forces of law and order and the way opened for reasonable discussion. Here it should be reiterated that the financial support of the IRA by some Americans is a grave disservice to the Irish people as a whole and that cutting the supply of funds from the United States would greatly help to bring peace to a troubled people.

There are some signs that the IRA now has far less support in all parts of Ireland than it has had for several years, and the spread of terrorist activity to England is widely interpreted as evidence of frustration at the failure of IRA tactics in Northern Ireland. But the possibility of finding a political solution to a centuries-old problem still seems remote, not least because the Protestant majority in Northern Ireland has been driven by recent events to a position of even greater intransigence. In these circumstances—and particularly if terrorist activity in England cannot be contained —the temptation will increase for the Westminster government to wash its hands of Northern Ireland and leave the rival groups to settle their differences in their own way. That is precisely what the terrorists are working for.

Already the majority of British people favor withdrawal, though there can be little doubt that an Irish civil war would result. So, again, the politicians have to take an unpopular stand, but—as in the case of capital punishment— they have the support of the British churches and indeed most of the more thoughtful elements in society as a whole.

III. THE STATE AS EXECUTIONER

EDITOR'S INTRODUCTION

In January of 1977 the state of Utah executed Gary Gilmore by firing squad for the crime of murder. The story—its drama heightened by last-minute stays, suicide attempts by Gilmore and by his lover Nicole Barrett, and his repeated insistence that he wanted to be put to death—had captured headlines for months. Groups opposed to the death penalty, such as the American Civil Liberties Union, worked literally up to the last minute to prevent the execution. However, after all legal recourse had been exhausted, the sentence was carried out—a way of settling the issue of Gilmore's crime, a way prescribed, or at least sanctioned, by the highest law in the land.

The first two articles in this section concern the Gilmore case. The opening article is a news report of the execution itself. The second selection presents a profile of the condemned man and traces some of his life history. Gary Gilmore was by no means unintelligent. In some respects he was sensitive and capable of concern. Yet he was sometimes uncontrollably violent and he could also kill without emotion. What is society to do with such a person?

The next article tells the story of this country's controversial death machine, the electric chair—its first use in the state of New York and some of its subsequent applications. The concluding selection recounts the historical events that led to the executions (for various crimes, but none of them murder) of a number of Americans, including the abolitionist John Brown and the labor leader Joe Hill.

GILMORE IS EXECUTED [1]

The ten-year suspension of capital punishment in the United States ended . . . [on January 17, 1977,] when four .30-caliber bullets ripped through the chest of Gary Mark Gilmore, the convicted killer who had asked the state of Utah to execute him.

The thirty-six-year-old Mr. Gilmore was put to death by a firing squad at 8:07 A.M. after a long, tension-filled night that had state lawyers flying in the predawn hours to Denver to overturn a stay of execution won hours earlier by foes of the death penalty.

When word arrived at the Utah State Prison here that the United States Court of Appeals for the Tenth Circuit had overturned the stay, the condemned murderer was taken from the maximum security section and was executed twenty minutes later in a cold and shadowy prison warehouse.

"Let's do it!" he said firmly when asked by Warden Samuel W. Smith if he had any last words.

Hood Placed Over His Head

Then, as thirty witnesses looked on and scraped their feet nervously on the gritty concrete floor of a storage area that had been cleared of paint drums and aluminum ladders, a black corduroy hood was slipped over the head of Mr. Gilmore, who sat strapped into a wooden chair on a makeshift platform raised one foot off the floor.

The officials stepped back, a signal was given and marksmen hidden behind an enclosed cubicle thirty feet away fired their rifles at the prisoner, who was bathed in light. His vital signs disappeared two minutes later, according to a medical examiner. . . .

An autopsy disclosed that all four bullets from the five

[1] From article entitled "Gilmore Is Executed After Stay Is Upset; 'Let's Do It!' He Said," by Jon Nordheimer, staff reporter. New York *Times*. p 1+. Ja. 18, '77. © 1977 by The New York Times Company. Reprinted by permission.

firing squad rifles—one was loaded with a blank—had pierced Mr. Gilmore's heart.

The dead man's eyes were removed for a cornea implant. The major organs, including the brain, were removed for medical study.

The body was removed to Provo, the scene of the shooting spree . . . [in 1976] that led to Mr. Gilmore's arrest and conviction, and plans were made for cremation. . . . The ashes of Gary Mark Gilmore, who sought solace in death after a violent life, will be scattered from a plane high above the rugged and timeless face of Utah.

The execution provoked an immediate reaction from capital punishment opponents across the land. But the most outraged came from representatives of the American Civil Liberties Union who worked feverishly over the last few days to halt the execution and in the early morning hours today believed that they had won.

Attorneys for the group obtained a ten-day restraining order from Federal District Judge Willis Ritter in Salt Lake City at 1:05 A.M., less than seven hours before Mr. Gilmore's scheduled execution at sunrise.

His decision was given in a class action suit that charged that the execution was an illegal expenditure of tax money because Utah's death penalty law was unconstitutional.

But lawyers from the office of Robert Hansen, the attorney general of Utah, seeking to bring the bizarre case to a conclusion, flew in a state plane to Denver to take the matter before the Appellate Court. In a special session of a panel of three circuit judges, Judge Ritter's decision was reversed.

While word of the decision was sent back to prison to proceed with the execution, the ACLU team, working through colleagues in Washington, made a desperate attempt to have the matter heard by the Supreme Court. However, the application was turned down by Associate Justices Thurgood Marshall and Byron R. White.

Three minutes later, Mr. Gilmore, who had openly

despised those who tried to save his life, was dead at 8:07. He was the first American on whom the death penalty was carried out since a Colorado man was executed in 1967.

Psychological Effect

Experts said that his execution would have little legal impact on the 354 other convicts under sentence of death but that the psychological impact of the ending of the moratorium should be great.

State officials were clearly concerned about more delays in the Gilmore case. There were two stays of execution at the end of 1976, and some people thought they were responsible for the prisoner's two attempts to take his own life.

When informed of the temporary stay in the middle of the night, Warden Smith said that the delays were placing extraordinary stress on a man who had been emotionally prepared, almost eager, to die for the last two months.

"If we have to execute him eventually, I'd as soon get it over with right now," said the warden, a laconic, 6-foot 6-inch Westerner. "I think [the delays] are very difficult things to impose on a person who's set his mind on execution. I think it's cruel and unusual punishment."

The warden, on orders from the attorney general's office, proceeded with the execution while aware that the petitioners were attempting to seek help from the Supreme Court. As it turned out, the request was denied three minutes before the execution took place, but the warden and the firing squad did not know the outcome when Mr. Gilmore was shot.

Gordon Richards, a law clerk in the attorney general's office who was at the execution, said that he had been instructed to wait one-half hour after notification of the reversal by the Circuit Court before allowing the execution to be carried out. He, too, acknowledged that the execution had taken place while the outcome of the appeal before the Supreme Court was still not known.

Mr. Gilmore, who was permitted to spend his last hours in the company of family members and his lawyers, apparently felt that way, too. He had approached his execution without apparent depression and little overt signs of tension, even dancing with his cousin and teaching his lawyers how to shadow box in the stark visitors' room where he was held on his last night.

Word of the "reprieve," however, caused him to explode with angry obscenities. He became so agitated that he was given additional sedatives.

No Sign of Delay

The night began without a sign that there was anything to block the sunrise execution. Courts on nearly every level in the state and federal systems had rejected petitions over the last several weeks by third parties attempting to block the execution after it had become apparent that the condemned man preferred a speedy death to prolonged imprisonment.

By the time the sun set yesterday, Mr. Gilmore's fate appeared sealed. Then came news of the restraining order, which set off a string of fast-breaking developments that kept everyone awake through the night, and each passing hour seemed to melt away the chances of an execution in the morning.

When dawn finally came, and the snow-rimmed peaks of the mountain ranges that border the Salt Lake Valley turned from pink to gold to white, the judge in the Gilmore trial altered his execution order to allow the state to put the prisoner to death after the original sunrise deadline.

When the phone call from Denver came, the prisoner was taken from the maximum security wing and transported across the frosty landscape to a one-level concrete block warehouse that formerly served as a cannery for the prison farm.

The prisoner, wearing a black T-shirt, white prison pants and tricolor tennis shoes, was ushered inside by guards and made to sit in a leather-backed wooden armchair just inside the door to the right. Behind the chair was a half-inch-thick plywood barrier, and behind that, against the gray concrete wall, were two piles of sandbags and a mattress with a soiled cover of blue and green flowered print.

Directly in front of the prisoner, ten yards away against the other wall, was the firing squad's cubicle, made of black muslin sheets suspended across a newly constructed frame of two-by-fours. On a horizontal line across the middle of the flimsy barrier, spaced every three feet, were five rectangular holes, each about three by six inches. At the extreme right was a smaller hole.

Strapped to the Chair

Mr. Gilmore was strapped loosely to the arms and legs of the chair as four witnesses he had asked to attend the execution were brought in, handed cotton for their ears and asked to stand off to the right behind a taped diagonal line on the floor. They were his two attorneys, Ron Stanger and Robert Moody; his uncle, Vern Damico, and the agent holding the motion picture and book rights to the doomed man's story, Lawrence Schiller.

The following account of the execution, which was completed within several minutes after the witnesses entered the long shed, was supplied by Mr. Schiller:

"There was the warden, a priest, a doctor and three or four others [prison officials] around him in red coats. To the left, behind a wooden barricade, there were approximately twenty other people.

"The warden asked Gary if he had any last words. Gary looked up for an extended period of time, then looked directly and said: 'Let's do it!'

"The priest and the doctor and several prison people placed a black hood over Gary. He did not quiver or deny its coverage. A black target with white circle was then pinned to Gary's black T-shirt. The priest and others moved away. Out of the corner of my eye, I believe the

warden gave some sort of signal. And then bang, bang, bang
—three noises in rapid succession. If there were four or
more [shots], then they overlapped."

POETRY OF A DOOMED CONVICT [2]

. . . [In 1974], locked in a prison cell in Oregon, Gary
Mark Gilmore wrote a poem that he called "The Land
Lord," and in it he presaged a coming rendezvous with
death.

Now behind bars in the Utah State Prison, asking the
state not to delay his scheduled execution for the July murder of a Provo motel manager, the thirty-five-year-old killer
is acting out his lyrical death vision.

He wrote years ago:

Feeling a beckoning wind blow through
The chambers of my soul   I knew
It was time I entered in.
I climbed within and stared about
It was home indeed
My very seed. . . .

Psychiatrists who have interviewed Mr. Gilmore since
his arrest . . . [in July 1976] for the murder in Provo and
the slaying a night earlier of a young gas station attendant
in Orem, have become convinced that when he was paroled
in Utah . . . he was a walking time bomb bent on self-de-
struction, calmly and coolly ticking toward an explosion
that was bound to take innocent lives.

The Gilmore case is destined to be argued in legal and
psychiatric circles as the nation prepares to resume the implementation of the death penalty after a long moratorium.

Giving the Job to Another

Central to the argument of whether capital punishment
is a deterrent or not is the category of killers who seem

[2] From article entitled "Death Wish Is Discerned in Poetry and Killings by
Doomed Convict," by Jon Nordheimer, staff correspondent. New York *Times.*
p 15. N. 15, '76. © 1976 by The New York Times Company. Reprinted by permission.

merely intoxicated by the prospect of their own punishment. These are, for the most part, men who have committed "senseless" crimes that outrage communities and excite a clamor for the death penalty.

"I think that shortly after Gary got out of prison he knew within himself that he was not able to make it in society," said Dr. John C. Woods, chief of forensic psychiatry at Utah State Hospital, who is one of the psychiatrists who examined the prisoner before his trial to determine if he were legally sane.

"Knowing he did not want to return to prison, he took the steps necessary to turn the job of his own destruction over to someone else," Dr. Woods theorized . . . in his office at the mental institution.

"He went out of his way to get the death penalty; that's why he pulled two execution-style murders he was bound to be caught for. I think it's a legitimate question, based on this evidence and our knowledge of the individual, to ask if Gilmore would have killed if there was not a death penalty in Utah."

A further extension of the argument, he added, raises the question of what the influence and the national publicity associated with the Gilmore case, in all its melodramatic aspect, will be on disturbed individuals who harbor the same obsessions.

"The trouble with the firing squad and hanging," said Dr. Woods, . . . "is that they have too much appeal to these disturbed minds. The glamour should be taken out of execution."

Effect of Publicity

The rush of publicity attending the case of the convict, who may become the first man to be legally executed since 1967 in the United States, has the potential to grow to carnival proportion. . . .

Few doubt the sincerity of his original declaration that he preferred a quick execution to months of legal delays or commutation of his sentence to life imprisonment. But now there are signs that he is sardonically enjoying the publicity that is being showered on him for the first time in a lifetime that has principally been spent behind bars.

Poet-killer, artist-thief, Gary Gilmore was deemed legally sane by the legal standards of the state, and is judged to be free of the profound psychoses that haunt many of those considered mentally ill.

For all but three of the last twenty-one years he has served time in correctional institutions, from reform school to federal maximum security prisons, and the long years have fashioned two sides to the same man.

One is a very bright . . . , sensitive and articulate individual who could have been a leader in society had his life gone another way. The other side of his personality is a "hardened, primitive sociopath," according to Dr. Woods, who said that Mr. Gilmore in his years inside the Oregon prison system had the reputation of a "cellblock enforcer, the king of the hill," a ruthless and moody convict. . . .

"I'm convinced he's killed before, both in and out of prison," Dr. Woods declared. "Sometimes individuals like Gilmore can't understand their own violence. It's the type of killer who turns real cold-blooded, not one who explodes with passion. For the protection of society I'm convinced we have to put such individuals away for life or execute them."

There is evidence the death wish started early in his life.

Mr. Gilmore's mother, who is a widow and runs a trailer park in Milwaukee, Oregon, had lived in Utah until she married an acrobat with a traveling circus. She went off to Texas, where Gary was born, and finally settled in Oregon, according to the convict's attorney, Dennis Boaz.

His father, now deceased, was an older man—forty-seven when Gary was born—a man described by his son as a charming hustler who was active in advertising in his later years, but also a distant parent given to violent periods of drunkenness, Mr. Boaz reported.

Resentful About Penitence

"Gary was rebellious at the Catholic parochial schools he attended," the lawyer continued. "He says he was very resentful about penitence and guilt, and how he hated it when the nuns made him write 'I will not make spitballs' five hundred times on the blackboard."

Those close to the case have seen evidence of a death wish in a small boy who had fantasies about his own execution, and in the adult convict who dreamed about his capacity to die according to the value system of the prison, the ability to catch and check the "red scream."

"These men tend to put up a brave front," said Dr. Roger Kieger, superintendent of the state hospital, who has closely observed condemned killers in Utah for twenty-three years, "but they are only covering up a lot of deep personal insecurity and fears of inadequacy."

The aura of quiet strength in the face of doom is carefully maintained.

. . . [On November 10, 1976] Mr. Boaz was with his client in the brightly lit maximum security section of the prison when a guard passed coffee to them and casually told them that the State Supreme Court had ruled that the condemned man could die tomorrow. That order was countermanded the next day by Governor Calvin L. Rampton's decision to allow the State Pardon Board to review the case. . . .

"Smiled at the News"

"Gary just smiled at the news," recalled Mr. Boaz, who is defending his client's claims to a right for a quick execution by the firing squad.

"You're a brave man," the lawyer told him.

"No one lives forever," the prisoner replied, still smiling. "This may sound strange, but I feel real good about it."

That night, on the prison's television screen, the inmates of death row watched the movie "Death Wish." Mr. Gilmore let it be known that his choice for the condemned man's traditional last meal was a six-pack of cold Coors beer.

"Gary's on a real macho trip, that's for sure," Mr. Boaz said later. "But he's not that cold-blooded. He tells me he feels guilt about the motel manager he killed, and his execution by the firing squad will help clear away his sins. He believes in karma, and that he will suffer pain for what he's done. He also believes in blood atonement, and that the soul evolves and there is reincarnation, and that the manner in which he dies can be a learning experience for others, to teach the other cons on death row courage and acceptance."

Had Other Choices Earlier

Death may be his last choice, but for a brief period . . . [in early 1976] after his release from prison, Gary Gilmore had been confronted with other choices.

He was a model parolee for the first month, electing to settle in Utah with distant relatives instead of returning to Oregon. An interesting component of this choice was that Oregon has no death penalty, while Utah has the firing squad, the only means of execution in the United States that sheds blood.

When he was a small boy, it now seems likely, he heard his mother's tales of her childhood in Utah, recalling that when a firing squad execution was scheduled, people from around the state would travel to Salt Lake City to witness it.

When Mr. Gilmore met Mrs. Barrett his life changed. He began drinking heavily, by his own admission, and when he drank he turned as violent as his father had. . . .

A psychiatrist close to the case wondered how a thirty-five-year-old man in prison with men for most of his adult life, exposed only to homosexual outlets, coped with challenges to his manhood.

"Always Enjoyed Women"

"I'm no Romeo but I've always enjoyed women," Mr. Gilmore has told his lawyer.

Nevertheless, the first murder took place on the night he and a woman checked into a room together at a Holiday Inn outside Provo. A gas station attendant was forced to lie on the floor and two bullets were fired into his head.

The next night brought Bennie Bushnell's time to die. He tried to evict Mr. Gilmore from the City Center Motel in Provo. He was slain in the same way.

"I didn't just kill him for the money," Mr. Gilmore later told his lawyer. "I just hate to be told what to do."

He did little to defend himself at his October [1975] trial. After his conviction and before the death sentence was passed, he told the jury that he had no choice but to kill Mr. Bushnell. "It was something that couldn't be stopped," he testified.

So it has all come down to a six-pack of beer and then the firing squad. . . .

To die like a man and to find peace at last, all images of the 1974 poem that ends:

> Borne aloft by a gray bat wing
> So many shadow images I met
> Myriad shapes, forms and phantoms of my being
> One thing was peculiar clear
> There was no scorn to menace here.
> This is just the way it is
> Laid bare to the bone
> And I built this house—I alone
> I am the Land Lord here.

THE ELECTRIC CHAIR [3]

In 1888, the New York legislature passed a law substituting electric shock for hanging as the state's official means of execution. This was a bold and perhaps rash innovation, as no one had ever been officially electrocuted and no one knew exactly how the new process would work.

Under the new law, effective January 1, 1889, the offices

[3] Article by Paul Meskil, journalist. Daily News. p 39. Ja. 7, '77. Copyright 1977 New York News, Inc. Reprinted by permission.

of the city and county executioners were abolished and the
state took over all executions within its borders. Electric
chairs were installed in Auburn, Clinton and Sing Sing
Prisons.

Willie Kemmler was the guinea pig chosen for the electric experiment that shocked the world.

Willie was a born loser. Two days after his marriage to
Ida Porter in Camden, New Jersey, he ran off with a married woman, Mrs. Tillie Ziegler. They settled in a Buffalo
slum, where Willie spent most of his time boozing, leaving
it to Tillie to provide what little money they had.

According to a newspaper article written in 1889, she
"supplemented her income in her own way." Whatever way
this was, Kemmler didn't approve. In a quarrel one night,
he split Tillie's skull with an axe. His murder trial took
only two days and ended in conviction. On May 14, 1889,
the judge sentenced him to die "by the application of electricity."

Hot Seat to Global Fame

The sentence jolted Willie from obscurity to global
fame. Many people felt that lightning bolts were the exclusive weapons of Mother Nature and should not be im-
itated by man. Many newspapers, politicians and clergymen
opposed electrocution. So did the electric companies, which
were trying at the time to convince the public that electricity was harmless.

When the state tried to purchase generators to power
its new death chairs, the electric companies refused to supply them. The state finally obtained the generators by or-
dering them through a dummy firm set up in Rio de
Janeiro.

Auburn Prison had been picked for the first electrocution. As soon as the generators arrived, a small army of
carpenters, electricians and other workers began building
the chair in a room near Willie's cell. He could hear them
talking, arguing, joking about the way he would burn.

A Sleepless Last Night

The execution was scheduled for the week of April 28, 1890, but the chair wasn't ready, so it was rescheduled for June and then for the week of August 2. Although the exact date was never announced, crowds began gathering outside the prison on August 5 and the warden decided not to disappoint them. Throughout the day and night, the workmen continued hammering, sawing, adjusting, testing the generator and voltmeter.

They made so much noise that Kemmler's last night of life was virtually sleepless. At 6 A.M. on August 6, a trusty delivered his breakfast. At 6:15, the warden delivered the death warrant. Willie put down the breakfast tray and accompanied the warden to the freshly painted death chamber.

The workers were still there and the twenty-one official witnesses—public officials, doctors, lawyers, lawmen and reporters—had arrived. The warden introduced Kemmler to the witnesses and asked if he had any last words.

"Well, gentlemen," Willie said, "I wish everyone good luck in this world and I think I am going to a good place and the papers have been saying a lot of stuff that isn't so. That's all I have to say."

Workmen were still tinkering with the strange contraption in the center of the room so Kemmler sat down on a small wooden chair and watched the final preparations for his doom.

When the workers finally departed, he walked calmly to the death chair. The warden nervously fastened the leather straps and tried to attach electrodes to his head and the base of his spine. "Keep cool, Warden," Willie advised. "Take your time. Do it well. Be sure everything's all right."

One of the witnesses, District Attorney Quinby of Buffalo, got up, left the room and fainted in the prison hallway. A deputy helped the warden fix the electrodes and the black hood. As they moved away from the chair, a guard

said "Goodbye, Willie" and knocked twice on the door to
an adjoining room, signaling the executioner. The switch
was pulled and the generator screamed like a fire siren.

Kemmler strained against the restraining straps, then
relaxed. After seventeen seconds, the current was turned off.
A physician examined Kemmler and had just pronounced
him dead when the corpse sighed. "He's still alive!" another
doctor shouted.

Several witnesses fainted. The electrodes were refastened
and the current was turned on again, for four seconds this
time, and, when it stopped, there was no doubt that the
electric chair was just as lethal as the hangman's rope.

Willie Kemmler was the first human to die in an electric
chair and the first of 695 condemned criminals—seven of
them women—to be electrocuted so far in New York State.

614 Sing Sing Sittings

There were 55 electrocutions at Auburn and 26 at Clinton before Sing Sing took over all state executions around
the turn of the century. The Sing Sing hot seat accommo-
dated 614 persons from 1891, when Harris A. Smiley died
for murdering Maggie Drainey, to 1963, when Eddie Lee
Mays was burned for the holdup murder of Marie Marini.
Mays was the last person executed in New York State.

Six years ago, the famous old Sing Sing chair was moved
to Green Haven Prison but it has not yet been used there.
Among its best-known customers were:

☐ Lieutenant Charles Becker, head of the Police Department's "strongarm squad." He hired four gunmen to
kill gambler Herman Rosenthal, who was talking about
police graft. Rosenthal was shot dead in 1912 outside the
Metropole Hotel, Broadway and 43d Street. The killers,
known as Gyp the Blood, Lefty Louie, Dago Frank and
Whitey Lewis, went to the chair the following year and
Becker was executed on July 30, 1915.

☐ Father Hans Schmidt, a Catholic priest who was de-
frocked in Germany for stealing church funds, then came

to America and continued working as a curate. He seduced and murdered a pretty German girl, Anna Aumueller, and threw her dismembered body into the Hudson. He went to the chair on February 18, 1916.

☐ Oresto Shillitani, twenty-four, who fatally shot a gangster and two cops on Mulberry Street in 1913. While awaiting execution, he somehow obtained a revolver and shot his way out of Death Row, killing one guard and wounding another before he was captured inside the prison. He was fried June 30, 1916.

☐ Louis (Lepke) Buchalter, boss of Murder Inc., the crime syndicate's killer corps. Lepke went to the chair March 4, 1944, with two of his henchmen, Louis Capone and Emmanuel (Mendy) Weiss. He was the only top executive of organized crime ever electrocuted.

☐ Martha Beck and Raymond Fernandez, the "Lonely Hearts Killers," who murdered two widows and a two-year-old girl. Two holdup killers, John King and Richard Powers, followed the gruesome couple to the chair on March 8, 1951, and the executioner picked up $600 ($150 a head) for the short night's work.

☐ Atom spies Julius and Ethel Rosenberg, executed June 19, 1953.

The electric chair was invented by Edward Davis, the state's chief executioner and first electrocutioner. He was succeeded by R. S. McNeal, who killed five men and one woman for a total pay of $100 before dropping dead in Auburn Prison.

Last Execution His Own

John Hulbert, a former assistant to Davis, took over the executioner's job on McNeal's death in 1913. Hulbert pulled the switch on 140 persons in New York and several other states before he retired in 1926.

"I got tired of killing people," he said when he quit in 1926.

But he performed one last execution. His own. On February 22, 1929, he took his old .38-caliber army revolver out of a trunk in the cellar of his modest home in Auburn, New York, and shot himself through the chest and brain.

His successor as state executioner, Robert Elliott, performed more than four hundred executions in six states—New York, New Jersey, Connecticut, Vermont, Massachusetts and Pennsylvania. Among his most famous victims were the anarchists Sacco and Vanzetti, executed for murder in Massachusetts [1927], and Bruno Richard Hauptmann, executed in New Jersey [1936] for the sensational kidnap murder of the Lindbergh baby.

A gaunt, grey man who lived in an unnumbered house . . . in Richmond Hill, Queens [New York City], Elliott ran a small electrical business in Queens to augment his state salary of $150 per execution. He died in bed of a heart attack on October 10, 1939.

Another electrician, Joseph Francel of Cairo, New York, succeeded Elliott and put 134 men and three women away in the Sing Sing chair, plus about 100 more in other states, in the fourteen years he held the job. In all those years, the state refused to raise his pay of $150 per execution. And that was why Francel resigned on August 15, 1953.

SOME HISTORIC EXECUTIONS [4]

On the night of May 24, 1856, a band of horsemen swooped down on a small farming settlement on Pottawatomie Creek, Kansas. They hauled the terrified settlers from their beds and murdered five men and boys.

Although none of the victims owned slaves, they had moved to Kansas from the South and were considered sympathetic to slavery. The midnight slaughter was led by John Brown and five of his sons.

A tall, bearded, wild-eyed fanatic, Brown was born in

---

[4] Article by Paul Meskil, journalist. *Daily News.* p 45. Ja. 6, '77. Copyright 1977 New York News, Inc., Reprinted by permission.

Torrington, Connecticut, in 1800. He grew up in Ohio, married twice, fathered 20 children and worked as a farmer, shepherd, wool merchant and leader of various anti-slavery groups. He became convinced that God had chosen him to abolish slavery.

"No political action will ever abolish the system of slavery," he said. "It will have to go out in blood."

Kansas Becomes Battleground

The Kansas-Nebraska Act of 1854 left it up to the residents to decide whether they wanted "free" or "slave" territories. Kansas promptly became a battleground for pro-slavery and abolitionist forces, with Brown and his oldest sons in the thick of the fray.

After the Pottawatomie Creek massacre, Brown took part in several armed skirmishes with slavery advocates and he became the hero of a group of militant Boston abolitionists. With their financial support, he planned a raid that would make history.

Brown and his twenty-one followers marched across the Potomac River into Harper's Ferry, Virginia, on the night of October 16, 1859. They cut the telegraph wires and seized the US arsenal. Brown was convinced all the slaves in the area would kill their owners and join him, but they didn't. The local militia stormed the arsenal and forced the raiders to retreat to a firehouse next door.

President James Buchanan sent a company of marines, under Colonel Robert E. Lee. Brown and his men greeted the marines with gunfire, but they had already suffered heavy casualties and soon were forced to surrender.

Before the battle of Harper's Ferry ended, eleven raiders, five civilians and one marine had been killed.

Refuses to Plead Insanity

One week after Brown surrendered, he was brought into the Jefferson County Courthouse in Charlestown, Virginia,

for arraignment on charges that he "did feloniously and
traitorously make rebellion and levy war" against the Commonwealth of Virginia. The trial began next day, but was
stalled by defense maneuvers. Brown's court-appointed lawyers urged him to plead insanity. He refused.

The nation's newspapers, even the abolitionist press, had
denounced the Harper's Ferry raid as the act of a madman.
But as the trial dragged on, sympathy for Brown spread
throughout the North and he was viewed as a courageous
crusader for freedom. The Virginia jury, however, found
him guilty and sentenced him to the gallows.

While he was in his cell, awaiting execution, he received
a letter from Mrs. Mahala Doyle, a widow, of Pottawatomie,
Kansas.

Altho' vengeance is not mine [she wrote], I confess that I do
feel gratified to hear that you were stopped in your fiendish
career at Harper's Ferry, with the loss of your two sons, you can
now appreciate my distress in Kansas when you then & there
entered my house at midnight and arrested my husband and two
boys, and took them out to the yard and in cold blood shot them
dead in my hearing. You can't say you done it to free slaves, we
had none and never expected to own one . . . O how it pained
my heart to hear the dying groans of my Husband & children, if
this scrawl gives you any consolation you are welcome to it.

Brown and five of his men were hanged on December 2,
1859, making him a martyr in the eyes of abolitionists and
bringing the nation a step closer to civil war.

Eight months later, the US warship Michigan stopped
the American cargo ship Erie about sixty miles off the
coast of Africa. A search of the merchantman revealed that
897 slaves were jammed between the decks. The Erie had
loaded its human cargo on the Congo River the day before
and was en route to Cuba when intercepted.

Piracy Charges

After rescuing the slaves and taking them home, the
Michigan escorted the Erie to New York and turned the

skipper, Captain Nathaniel Gordon, over to federal authorities on piracy charges. Gordon, twenty-eight, of Portland, Maine, was the son of a merchant marine captain and had spent most of his life at sea.

The jury at his first trial in Manhattan Federal Court was unable to reach a verdict. His second trial began November 6, 1861. By now, the country was at war and anti-slavery sentiment in the North was at its peak. Gordon was convicted and sentenced to hang.

Before signing the death warrant, Judge Shipman told the prisoner:

Think of the cruelty and wickedness of seizing nearly a thousand human beings, who never did you any harm, and thrusting them between the decks of a small ship, beneath a burning tropical sun, to die of disease or suffocation, or to be transported to distant lands and consigned, they and their posterity, to a fate far more cruel than death.

The execution was finally scheduled for February 21, 1862. On the night of February 20, Gordon's wife and mother visited him in his cell. . . . After they left, he smoked several cigars and retired at 1:30 A.M.

Around 3 A.M., a guard looked into the cell and saw that Gordon was suffering from severe convulsions. The prison physician examined him and said he had taken poison, probably strychnine concealed in the cigars. Two other doctors were summoned. They worked on him for five hours with a stomach pump and doses of brandy. Finally they brought him back from the brink of death.

The execution had been scheduled for 2 P.M., but United States Marshal Murray moved it up to noon because he feared Gordon might suffer a relapse and beat the hangman.

At 11 A.M., a company of marines entered the prison yard, carrying muskets with fixed bayonets. A marine band accompanied them and played military marches as the executioner tested the scaffold and gallows.

Requests Reprieve

At 11:15, Gordon's lawyer arrived and asked Murray to delay the execution because Governor Morgan had sent a telegram to President Lincoln, requesting a reprieve. Murray refused. At the stroke of noon, the marshal entered Gordon's cell and told him it was time to go.

Gordon asked for something to drink. He was given a bottle of brandy. In the next few minutes, he gulped down three or four glasses of brandy and became so unsteady that two deputy marshals had to support him on the walk to the scaffold.

As the black cap of death was being placed over his head, he either fainted or passed out. Deputies grabbed him and held him erect until the rope yanked him into the air.

He was the only person ever executed in the United States for engaging in the slave trade.

After the Civil War, a bitter struggle began between workers and factory-owners. Labor unions were organized to demand higher pay, shorter hours and better working conditions. Anarchists tried to incite the workers to violence. Strikes closed industrial plants all over the country.

On May 4, 1886, a labor rally was held in Chicago's Haymarket Square to protest a police strike-breaking foray in which one striker was shot dead and several others were wounded. The rally was peaceful, but a police captain decided to break it up and sent 180 cops into the square.

Someone tossed a dynamite bomb into the bluecoat ranks killing seven policemen and wounding sixty-six.

Eight anarchists were arrested, tried and convicted of conspiring to commit murder, although there was no evidence that any of them threw the bomb or knew who did. Seven of the defendants were sentenced to death; the eighth was given a fifteen-year prison term.

Blows Himself Up

Illinois Governor Richard Oglesby later commuted the death sentences of Samuel Fielden and Michael Schwab to life imprisonment. Another convicted anarchist, Louis Lingg, blew himself up with a bomb that was smuggled into his cell.

The remaining four condemned men—August Spies, George Engels, Albert Parsons and Adolph Fischer—went to the gallows on November 11, 1887, amid a public outcry that echoed around the world.

Next year, the new governor of Illinois, John Peter Altgeld, pardoned the three surviving anarchists and denounced the judge and jury that sentenced them. "The trial was not fair," he said.

Shortly before the outbreak of World War I, American union members were singing a song called "The Preacher and the Slave." The lyrics were somewhat simplistic: Work and pray/Live on hay/You'll get pie/In the sky/When you die/It's a lie."

The author was a union organizer known as Joe Hill. Born . . . in Sweden, he emigrated to the United States around the turn of the century . . . and eventually joined the Industrial Workers of the World, which was called the Wobblies.

Convicted of armed robbery, Joe Hill was executed by a Utah firing squad on November 19, 1915. His friends and supporters maintained he was framed. He became a martyr of the labor movement and the hero of the folk ballad "I Thought I Saw Joe Hill Last Night."

IV. LIFE OR DEATH

EDITOR'S INTRODUCTION

This section sums up the arguments for and against the death penalty. There is much to be thought about on both sides and the debate will probably never be settled.

The first article, by a former associate justice of the United States Supreme Court, offers a strong argument against capital punishment. Abe Fortas contends that the pointless exercise of executing a few people each year degrades and brutalizes our civilization. He concludes with the hope that this country will reject killing as a means of law enforcement.

The selection that follows is written by a former attorney general of the United States, Ramsey Clark. He also comes out strongly against the death penalty. Examining the deterrent effect of the death penalty, he finds it largely illusory. More must be done, he says, to rehabilitate the criminal. If the offender is judged to be a continuing danger to the community, he can always be kept in prison.

The third article presents the case for capital punishment, favoring retention of the death penalty because it is consistent with a concern for human life—the life of the victim. The article suggests that there is indeed a deterrent effect of the supreme punishment and that under prescribed conditions it is a useful tool of law.

The address that follows asks the question, Who speaks for the victims of crime in America? The author, a former attorney general of the state of Indiana, states that if capital punishment were to be made the sure result of conviction for certain types of murder, society as a whole would benefit.

Concern for the victims of crime is on the increase, especially concern for the truly defenseless—the old and the very young. There is a call for more severe punishment, possibly even mandatory punishment, for those committing such crimes. Would this be considered discriminatory?

The next article contains a question-and-answer debate on some of the issues surrounding the death penalty, among them discriminatory application of the sentence, the so-called deterrent effect, and the "cruel and unusual" nature of the punishment. Covering the same ground, the two participants, Ernest van den Haag, a psychoanalyst, and Louis B. Schwartz, a law professor, reach diametrically opposed conclusions.

The sixth article, an editorial in the *National Review,* argues that deterrence is not sufficient justification for capital punishment—yet some crimes may *deserve* execution.

The last selection presents the entire debate over capital punishment as an exercise in logic. Neither favoring nor opposing the death penalty, Professor James Q. Wilson, Shattuck Professor of Government at Harvard, examines the most commonly used arguments on both sides and concludes that the real question is one of justice: whether capital punishment can be regarded as a fitting penalty for certain crimes. Such a question forces us to balance respect for life with abhorrence of crime. It requires that our consideration of the death penalty go beyond matters of deterrence, capriciousness, discrimination, or cruelty to the ultimate issue of human values.

THE CASE AGAINST
CAPITAL PUNISHMENT [1]

I believe that most Americans, even those who feel it is necessary, are repelled by capital punishment; the attitude is deeply rooted in our moral reverence for life, the Judeo-Christian belief that man is created in the image of God. Many Americans were pleased when on June 29, 1972, the Supreme Court of the United States set aside death sen-

[1] From article by Abe Fortas, former associate justice, United States Supreme Court. New York *Times Magazine.* p 8+. Ja. 23, '77. © 1977 by The New York Times Company. Reprinted by permission.

tences for the first time in its history. On that day the Court handed down its decision in *Furman v. Georgia,* holding that the capital-punishment statutes of three states were unconstitutional because they gave the jury complete discretion to decide whether to impose the death penalty or a lesser punishment in capital cases. For this reason, a bare majority of five justices agreed that the statutes violated the "cruel and unusual punishment" clause of the Eighth Amendment.

The result of this decision was paradoxical. Thirty-six states proceeded to adopt new death-penalty statutes designed to meet the Supreme Court's objection, and beginning in 1974, the number of persons sentenced to death soared. In 1975 alone, 285 defendants were condemned— more than double the number sentenced to death in any previously reported year. Of those condemned in 1975, 93 percent had been convicted of murder; the balance had been convicted of rape or kidnapping.

The constitutionality of these death sentences and of the new statutes, however, was quickly challenged, and on July 2, 1976, the Supreme Court announced its rulings in five test cases. It rejected "mandatory" statutes that automatically imposed death sentences for defined capital offenses, but it approved statutes that set out "standards" to guide the jury in deciding whether to impose the death penalty. These laws, the court ruled, struck a reasonable balance between giving the jury some guidance and allowing it to take into account the background and character of the defendant and the circumstances of the crime.

The decisions may settle the basic constitutional issue until there is a change in the composition of the Court, but many questions remain. Some of these are questions of considerable constitutional importance, such as those relating to appellate review. Others have to do with the sensational issues that accompany capital punishment in our society. Gary Gilmore generated an enormous national debate by insisting on an inalienable right to force the people of Utah to kill him. So did a district judge who ruled that television may present to the American people the spectacle of a man being electrocuted by the state of Texas.

The recent turns of the legislative and judicial process have done nothing to dispose of the matter of conscience and judgment for the individual citizen. The debate over it will not go away; indeed, it has gone on for centuries.

Through the years, the number of offenses for which the state can kill the offender has declined. Once, hundreds of capital crimes, including stealing more than a shilling from a person and such religious misdeeds as blasphemy and witchcraft, were punishable by death. But in the United States today, only two principal categories remain—major assaults upon persons, such as murder, kidnapping, rape, bombing and arson, and the major political crimes of espionage and treason. In addition, there are more than twenty special capital crimes in some of our jurisdictions, including train robbery and aircraft piracy. In fact, however, in recent years murder has accounted for about 90 percent of the death sentences and rape for most of the others, and the number of states prescribing the death penalty for rape is declining.

At least forty-five nations, including most of the Western democracies, have abolished or abandoned capital punishment. Ten US states have no provision for the death penalty. In four, the statutes authorizing it have recently been declared unconstitutional under state law. The Federal Criminal Code authorizes capital punishment for various offenses, but there have been no executions under federal civil law (excluding military jurisdiction) since the early 1960s.

Public-opinion polls in our nation have seesawed, with some indication that they are affected by the relative stability or unrest in our society at the time of polling. In 1966, a public-opinion poll reported that 42 percent of the American public favored capital punishment, 47 percent opposed it and 11 percent were undecided. In 1972-1973,

both the Gallup and Harris polls showed that 57 percent
to 59 percent of the people favored capital punishment,
and a recent Gallup poll asserts that 65 percent favor it.

Practically all scholars and experts agree that capital
punishment cannot be justified as a significantly useful
instrument of law enforcement or of penology. There is no
evidence that it reduces the serious crimes to which it is
addressed. Professor William Bowers, for example, concludes in his excellent study *Executions in America* that
statutory or judicial developments that change the risk of
execution are not paralleled by variations in homicide
rates. He points out that over the last thirty years, homicide
rates have remained relatively constant while the number
of executions has steadily declined. He concludes that the
"death penalty, as we use it, exerts no influence on the extent or rate of capital offenses." [For opposite point of view
see article by Theodore Sendak below in this Section.—Ed.]

I doubt that fear of the possible penalty affects potential
capital offenders. The vast majority of capital offenses are
murders committed in the course of armed robbery that
result from fear, tension or anger of the moment, and murders that are the result of passion or mental disorder. The
only deterrence derived from the criminal process probably
results from the fear of apprehension and arrest, and possibly from the fear of significant punishment. There is little,
if any, difference between the possible deterrent effect of
life imprisonment and that of the death penalty.

The Infrequency of Execution

In fact, the statistical possibility of execution for a capital offense is extremely slight. We have not exceeded one
hundred executions a year since 1951, although the number
of homicides in death-sentence jurisdictions alone has
ranged from 7,500 to 10,000. In 1960, there were only fifty-
six executions in the United States, and the number declined each year thereafter. . . . In the peak year of 1933,
there were only 199 executions in the United States, while

the average number of homicides in all of the states authorizing capital punishment for 1932-33 was 11,579.

A potential murderer who rationally weighed the possibility of punishment by death (if there is such a person), would figure that he has considerably better than a 98 percent chance of avoiding execution in the average capital-punishment state. In the years from 1960 to 1967, his chances of escaping execution were better than 99.5 percent. The professional or calculating murderer is not apt to be deterred by such odds.

An examination of the reason for the infrequency of execution is illuminating:

1. Juries are reluctant to condemn a human being to death. The evidence is that they are often prone to bring in a verdict of a lesser offense, or even to acquit, if the alternative is to impose the death penalty. The reluctance is, of course, diminished when powerful emotions come into play—as in the case of a black defendant charged with the rape of a white woman.

2. Prosecutors do not ask for the death penalty in the case of many, perhaps a majority, of those who are arrested for participation in murder or other capital offenses. In part, this is due to the difficulty of persuading juries to impose death sentences; in part, it is due to plea bargaining. In capital cases involving more than one participant, the prosecutor seldom asks for the death penalty for more than one of them. Frequently, in order to obtain the powerful evidence necessary to win a death sentence, he will make a deal with all participants except one. The defendants who successfully "plea bargain" testify against the defendant chosen for the gallows and in return receive sentences of imprisonment.

This system may be defensible in noncapital cases because of practical exigencies, but it is exceedingly disturbing where the result is to save the witness's life at the hazard of the life of another person. The possibility is obvious that the defendant chosen for death will be selected on a basis that has nothing to do with comparative guilt, and the danger is inescapable that the beneficiary of the plea-bargain, in order to save his life, will lie or give distorted testimony. . . .

3. As a result of our doubts about capital punishment, and our basic aversion to it, we have provided many escape hatches. Every latitude is allowed the defendant and his counsel in the trial; most lawyers representing a capital offender quite properly feel that they must exhaust every possible defense, however technical or unlikely; appeals are generally a matter of right; slight legal errors, which would be disregarded in other types of cases, are grounds for reversal; governors have, and liberally exercise, the power to commute death sentences. Only the rare, unlucky defendant is likely to be executed when the process is all over.

In 1975, sixty-five prisoners on death row had their death-penalty status changed as a result of appeals, court actions, commutation, resentencing, etc. This was more than 20 percent of the new death-row prisoners admitted during that peak year.

It is clear that American prosecutors, judges and juries are not likely to cause the execution of enough capital offenders to increase the claimed deterrent effect of capital-punishment laws or to reduce the "lottery" effect of freakish selection. People generally may favor capital punishment in the abstract, but pronouncing that a living person shall be killed is quite another matter. Experience shows that juries are reluctant to order that a person be killed. Where juries have been commanded by law to impose the death penalty, they have often chosen to acquit or, in modern times, to convict of a lesser offense rather than to return a verdict that would result in execution.

The Inequalities of the Law

The law is a human instrument administered by a vast number of different people in different circumstances, and we are inured to its many inequalities. Tweedledee may be imprisoned for five years for a given offense, while Tweedledum, convicted of a similar crime, may be back on the streets in a few months. We accept the inevitability of such discriminations, although we don't approve of them, and we constantly seek to reduce their frequency and severity. But the taking of a life is different from any other punishment. It is final; it is ultimate; if it is erroneous, it is irreversible and beyond correction. . . .

We have gone a long way toward recognition of the unique character of capital punishment. We insist that it be imposed for relatively few crimes of the most serious nature and that it be imposed only after elaborate precautions to reduce the possibility of error. We also inflict it in a fashion that avoids the extreme cruelty of such methods as drawing and quartering, though it still involves the barbaric rituals attendant upon electrocution, the gallows or the firing squad.

But fortunately, the death penalty is and will continue to be sought in only a handful of cases and rarely carried out. So long as the death penalty is a highly exceptional punishment, it will serve no deterrent or penological function; it will fulfill no pragmatic purpose of the state; and inevitably, its selective imposition will continue to be influenced by racial and class prejudice.

All of the standards that can be written, all of the word magic and the procedural safeguards that can be devised to compel juries to impose the death penalty on capital offenders without exception or discrimination will be of no avail. In a 1971 capital-punishment case, [Supreme Court] Justice John Harlan wrote on the subject of standards.

They do no more [he said] than suggest some subjects for the jury to consider during its deliberations, and [the criteria] bear witness to the intractable nature of the problem of "standards" which the history of capital punishment has from the beginning reflected.

Form and substance are important to the life of the law, but when the law deals with a fundamental moral and constitutional issue—the disposition of human life—the use of such formulas is not an acceptable substitute for a correct decision on the substance of the matter.

The discrimination that is inescapable in the selection of the few to be killed under our capital-punishment laws is unfortunately of the most invidious and unacceptable sort. Most of those who are chosen for extinction are black (53.5 percent in the years 1930 to 1975). The wheels of chance and prejudice begin to spin in the police station; they continue through the prosecutor's choice of defendants for whom he will ask the death penalty and those he will choose to spare; they continue through the trial and in the jury room, and finally they appear in the governor's office. Solemn "presumptions of law" that the selection will be made rationally and uniformly violate human experience and the evidence of the facts. Efforts to bring about equality of sentence by writing "standards" or verbal formulas may comfort the heart of the legislator or jurist, but they can hardly satisfy his intelligence.

If deterrence is not a sufficient reason to justify capital-punishment laws and if their selective application raises such disturbing questions, what possible reason is there for their retention? One other substantive reason, advanced by eminent authorities, is that the execution of criminals is justifiable as "retribution." This is the argument that society should have the right to vent its anger or abhorrence against the offender, that it may justifiably impose a punishment people believe the criminal "deserves." Albert Camus [Nobel prize winning French author], in a famous essay, says of capital punishment: "Let us call it by the name which, for lack of any other nobility, will at least give the nobility of truth, and let us recognize it for what it is essentially: a revenge."

We may realize that deep-seated emotions underlie our capital-punishment laws, but there is a difference between our understanding of the motivation for capital punishment and our acceptance of it as an instrument of our society. We may appreciate that the *lex talionis*, the law of revenge, has its roots in the deep recesses of the human spirit, but that awareness is not a permissible reason for retaining capital punishment.

Capital Punishment an Ancient Sanction

It is also argued that capital punishment is an ancient sanction that has been adopted by most of our legislatures after prolonged consideration and reconsideration, and that we should not override this history.

But the argument is not persuasive. If we were to restrict the implementation of our Bill of Rights, by either constitutional decisions or legislative judgments, to those practices that its provisions contemplated in 1791, we would indeed be a retarded society. In 1816, Thomas Jefferson wrote a letter in which he spoke of the need for constitutions as well as other laws and institutions to move forward "hand in hand with the progress of the human mind." . . .

As early as 1910, the Supreme Court, in the case of *Weems v. United States,* applied this principle to a case in which the defendant had been sentenced to fifteen years in prison for the crime of falsifying a public document as part of an embezzlement scheme. The Court held that the sentence was excessive and constituted "cruel and unusual punishment" in violation of the Eighth Amendment. In a remarkable opinion, Justice Joseph McKenna eloquently rejected the idea that prohibitions of the Bill of Rights, including the Eighth Amendment, must be limited to the practices to which they were addressed in 1791, when the great amendments were ratified. He said:

Time works changes, brings into existence new conditions and purposes. Therefore a principle, to be vital, must be capable of wider application than the mischief which gave it birth. This is peculiarly true of constitutions. They are not ephemeral enactments, designed to meet passing occasions.

As to the "cruel and unusual punishment" clause of the Constitution, he said that it "is not fastened to the obsolete, but may acquire meaning as public opinion becomes enlightened by a humane justice."

We have also long recognized that the progressive implementation of the Bill of Rights does not depend upon first obtaining a majority vote or a favorable Gallup or Harris poll. . . .

Indeed, despite our polls, public opinion is unfathomable; . . . and if known, no one can predict how profound or shallow it is as of the moment, and how long it will persist. Basically, however, the obligation of legislators and judges who question whether a law or practice is or is not consonant with our Constitution is inescapable; it cannot be delegated to the Gallup poll, or to the ephemeral evidence of public opinion.

We will not eliminate the objections to capital punishment by legal legerdemain, by "standards," by procedures or by word formulas. The issue is fundamental. It is wrong for the state to kill offenders; it is a wrong far exceeding the numbers involved. In exchange for the pointless exercise of killing a few people each year, we expose our society to brutalization; we lower the essential value that is the basis of our civilization: a pervasive, unqualified respect for life. And we subject ourselves and our legal institutions to the gross spectacle of a pageant in which death provides degrading, distorting excitement. . . .

Beyond all of these factors is the fundamental consideration: In the name of all that we believe in and hope for, why must we reserve to ourselves the right to kill one hundred or two hundred people? Why, when we can point to no tangible benefit; why, when in all honesty we must admit that we are not certain that we are accomplishing anything except serving the cause of "revenge" or retribution?

Why, when we have bravely and nobly progressed so far in the recent past to create a decent, humane society, must we perpetuate the senseless barbarism of official murder? . . .

I hope and believe we will conclude that the time has come for us to join the company of those nations that have repudiated killing as an instrument of criminal law enforcement.

THE DEATH PENALTY AND
REVERENCE FOR LIFE [2]

More than seventy nations and thirteen American states have acted to reduce human violence by abolishing the death penalty. Among advanced nations the United States remains the chief advocate of death as a punishment for crime. We are characterized in the eyes of millions as much by our executions as by the general violence of our environment. Indeed, the two phenomena blur into one. The inhumanity of Vietnam and the death there inflicted further persuade the citizens of many nations that Americans are a violent, a dangerous, people.

Most of our states and the federal government itself reserve the right to kill and actually impose the death penalty, though it has been rarely exercised in recent years. Compared to 199 executions in the United States in 1935, there were but one in 1966 and two in 1967. There were none . . . [from 1968 through 1976]. Only one person has been executed in the past decade under the twenty-nine federal statutes authorizing death, and no life has been taken by federal justice since 1963. [In January 1977, Gary Gilmore was executed by firing squad in Utah after much legal wrangling. See "Gilmore Is Executed," by Jon Nordheimer, in Section III, above.—Ed.] Still, as the 1960s closed, more than 500 men waited under sentence of death while

[2] From *Crime in America*, by Ramsey Clark, former attorney general of the United States, Simon & Schuster, '70; Pocket Books. '71. p 308-15. Copyright © 1970 by Ramsey Clark. Reprinted by permission of Simon & Schuster, Inc.

the Supreme Court reviewed cases which challenged the constitutionality of capital punishment.

History shows that the death penalty has been unjustly imposed—innocents have been killed by the state, effective rehabilitation has been impaired, judicial administration has suffered—and crime has not been deterred. Our emotions may cry for vengeance in the wake of a horrible crime, but we know that killing the criminal cannot undo the crime, will not prevent similar crimes by others, does not benefit the victim, destroys human life, and brutalizes society. If we are to still violence, we must cherish life. Executions cheapen life.

The major argument for capital punishment today is the belief that fear of death will keep people from committing serious crimes. But most studies of the death penalty have concluded with Professor Thorsten Sellin that "it has failed as a deterrent." A comprehensive United Nations report found that abolition of the death penalty has no effect on murder rates. With or without capital punishment, murder rates are much the same. [For information supportive of the deterrent theory, see "Deterrent Effect of Capital Punishment," by Issac Ehrlich in *American Economic Review,* June 1975.—Ed.]

Why should we expect a deterrent value? Do we really believe most capital crimes are rational acts? Are they not more often committed on impulse—in a moment of passion—without thought of gain or loss? Only extreme fear of punishment—so emotionally severe that basic instincts are cowed—can deter unpremeditated crime. It is, after all, meditation before the act that may cause a person aware of the risks and consequences of being caught to refrain from prohibited conduct.

Premeditated crime, in the view of scholarship on the subject, is committed by people who believe they will not be caught. They do not really weigh the penalty. If this is so, the best deterrent for premeditated crime is to give potential offenders cause to believe they will be caught and proven guilty. Swift apprehension, effective prosecution and quick conviction will do this. When these are achieved, people can see that in fact they are paying society's price. Professionally trained police, the application of science and technology to criminal justice, successful prosecution and speedy trials can thus prevent violence—while capital punishment only makes crime a more deadly game.

The hardened criminal, devoid of human compassion, will not be deterred by the fear of death or severe punishment. He lives among the springs of American violence, where sudden death is no stranger. Society must protect itself by rehabilitating him or isolating him. To seek some public satisfaction from his execution will only brutalize others.

George Bernard Shaw believed, "Murder and capital punishment are not opposites that cancel one another, but similars that breed their kind." His view has scientific basis. The death penalty is observed by many psychologists to be an incentive for some mentally unstable persons to commit capital crimes. Recognizing the high correlation between murder and emotional disturbance, as well as a psychotic compulsion to gain notoriety, to shock sensitive people and to injure oneself, they see the death penalty as a cause of serious crime. Unquestionably, it has this effect on some. Just as arson, assassination, murder and rape inspire others who hear of them to consider and sometimes commit similar crimes, the news of executions affects mentally disturbed people, who have been known to emulate the offenses of the condemned. . . .

The death penalty causes violence in many ways. The effect of executions on other inmates in a prison where the condemned wait to die is devastating. The "big houses," major penitentiaries where the executions usually occur, frequently confine several thousand men. They are the most dangerous offenders convicted of crime, many deeply disturbed emotionally. Inmates there are constantly aware of the men on death row. Seeing them wait month after month, they wonder what kind of people we are. What kind of game this is we play—as if society were a giant cat and the condemned man a mouse to be toyed with before being killed. Even when prisoners who have lived in the presence of the condemned are released—and nearly all are—we know most will be convicted of crime again, because we fail to give them a chance. For how many of those later released has the final image before pulling the trigger of a pistol pointed at a police officer been the eyes of the men on death row and the thought, not me? . . .

Wardens and guards are deeply affected by death row. The ugly details—the last meal, clothing that will not retain poisonous gas, the frequent failures on first attempt, the fear that a last-minute commutation may come too late, working with warm flesh that knows it is about to die—are not pleasant experiences. The roll of wardens who have spoken out strongly against capital punishment is long. . . . They know the inhumanity of the death penalty and the effect of execution on the other men in their custody.

Capital punishment harms everything it touches. The impact of the death penalty on the administration of justice has been terribly damaging. Lawyers have long noted that hard cases make bad law. There are few cases harder than those which take a life. [Supreme Court] Justice Felix Frankfurter strongly opposed capital punishment for this reason. "When life is at hazard in a trial," he said, "it sensationalizes the whole thing almost unwittingly." He regarded the effect on juries, the bar, the public and the judiciary as "very bad." President [Lyndon B.] Johnson's Crime Commission found that the emotion surrounding a capital case "destroys the fact-finding process." Realization of the consequences of error permeates the entire proceeding. A jury may acquit because of its fear of the death penalty when the evidence clearly establishes guilt of a serious crime. . . .

Fear of mistake produces excruciating delays in executions. In the late 1960s there were more than four hundred persons on death row at all times. Most spent years in the shadow of death. Their ages ranged from fifteen to seventy. The unbearably long wait adds immeasurably to the inhumanity of capital punishment and, combined with the infrequency of actual execution, eliminates the one deterrent effect the penalty might otherwise be thought to have. The punishment is not only slow; it usually never comes.

In a 1961 study the American Bar Foundation found that long delays such as those in the Caryl Chessman case weaken public confidence in the law. [See "Above and Beyond Capital Punishment," by George Stevens, in Section I, above.] This is an understatement born of self-interest. Such cases have disgusted millions. In a more outspoken vein, the President's Crime Commission noted: "The spectacle of men living on death row for years while their lawyers pursue appellate and collateral remedies, tarnishes our image of humane and expeditious justice."

We torture ourselves through delay, indecision and doubt because we do not really believe in taking human life. No one in the process feels comfortable with himself, or about his government. The resulting hesitation further heightens the harm of the penalty. This is part of the price of hypocrisy.

History is full of men who have opposed capital punishment. . . . Fear of error has caused many to oppose capital punishment. It should. Innocent persons have been executed. In addition, some incapable of knowing what they did—the mentally retarded and disturbed—have been sacrificed to our lust for punishment and vengeance. Judicial determination of mental competence, a prerequisite to a finding that a person is legally responsible for a criminal act, remains far from a precise science. The legal standards are neither clear nor sound, and the decisions are made in emotional contexts. But fear of a mistake, that the person was innocent or knew not what he did, ignores the greater reason for abolition. We must be humane.

Death has been visited in a discriminatory fashion. A small group of offenders selected by chance have been destroyed. Most who committed similar crimes were never caught. Nearly all of the persons caught and convicted of the same crimes for which a few were killed have been imprisoned—not executed. There are thousands of prisoners serving life sentences or less whose crimes were more inhumane than those of the men on death row.

The poor and the black have been the chief victims of the death penalty. . . . It is the poor, the sick, the ignorant, the powerless and the hated who are executed.

Racial discrimination is manifest from the bare statistics of capital punishment. Since we began keeping records in 1930, there have been 2,066 Negroes and only 1,751 white persons put to death. Negroes have been only one-eighth of our population. Hundreds of thousands of rapes have occurred in America since 1930, yet only 455 men have been executed for rape—and 405 of them were Negroes. There can be no rationalization or justification of such clear discrimination. It is outrageous public murder, illuminating our darkest racism.

Why must we kill? We are finally beginning to realize that crime is preventable and rehabilitation possible. The medical sciences, psychiatry, psychology, sociology, education, training and employment can prevent crime. Modern penology offers effective methods of protecting society. Predelinquency guidance and assistance, treatment centers, halfway houses and work release programs are evidence of the movement toward community programs that offer so much. They are the future of corrections. It is a sad commentary on how much we care that this wealthy nation spends 95 percent of all funds for corrections on pure custody and only 5 percent on hope—health services, education, employment and rehabilitation techniques—while still killing those who offend it the most.

If an offender cannot adapt to community programs, he can be retained in prison. If he is dangerous, he can be prevented from doing injury. Through employment in industries within the prison he can be productive. If he is unable or unwilling to work, he can still be treated kindly and allowed to live. Society can be fully protected. We no longer need to kill from fear.

Murderers, the persons for whom the death penalty is most frequently invoked, generally make well-behaved prisoners. They are rarely a threat to the safety of others. A study during the 1940s of 121 assaults with intent to kill in the prisons of twenty-seven states showed that only 10 were committed by prisoners serving life sentences for murder. There is nothing in prison experience to indicate that the death penalty would protect prison personnel from assaults by life-termers, whatever their earlier crime.

The death penalty is inconsistent with the purposes of modern penology. It deters rehabilitation. It is a disastrous substitute for the effort and money needed to develop correctional knowledge and skills.

Surely the abolition of the death penalty is a major milestone in the long road up from barbarism. There were times when self-preservation may have necessitated its imposition. Later, when food, clothing and shelter were scarce and often insufficient, inordinate sacrifices by the innocent would have been required to isolate dangerous persons from the public. Our civilization has no such excuse.

There is no justification for the death penalty. It demeans life. Its inhumanity raises basic questions about our institutions and our purpose as a people. Why must we kill? What do we fear? What do we accomplish besides our own embitterment? We must revere life and in so doing create in the hearts of our people a love for mankind that will finally still violence. A humane and generous concern for every individual, for his safety, his health and his fulfillment, will do more to soothe the savage heart than the fear of state-inflicted death, which chiefly serves to remind us how close we remain to the jungle. So long as government takes the life of its citizens, the mandate "Thou shalt not kill" will never have the force of the absolute. Our greatest need is reverence for life—mere life, all life—life as an end in itself.

IN THE INTEREST OF LIFE [3]

I am sure that most persons who urge legislation to abolish capital punishment do so because of a concern for human life. It is precisely for this reason that I urge in favor of recommending a retention of this form of crime prevention.

The logic which urges an abolition of the death penalty in the interest of human life is more apparent than real. For I am convinced that ultimately abolition of capital punishment would result in a much greater loss of human life than would its retention.

It is admittedly tragic whenever the state in the most awesome exercise of its authority decides that capital punishment must be invoked, tragic because any loss of human life is a tragedy. But I submit to you that even in the tragedy of human death there are degrees, and that it is much more tragic for the innocent to lose his life than for the state to take the life of a criminal convicted of a capital offense.

My statement implies a belief that there is a direct relationship between the legal existence of capital punishment and the incidence of criminal homicide. Although statistics are generally unreliable in this area, I am convinced that such a relationship does exist. I am convinced that many potential murderers are deterred simply by their knowledge that capital punishment exists, and may be their fate if they commit the crime they contemplate.

I think it significant that during recent years we have seen a consistent reduction in the number of incidents of

[3] Excerpt by Glen D. King, director, Information Service Division, International Association of Chiefs of Police, taken from, "Controversy Over the Question of Capital Punishment in the U.S." *Congressional Digest.* 52:15+. Ja. '73. Reprinted by permission.

capital punishment, and at the same time a very great increase in the number of criminal homicides.

As an example, in 1950, 82 convicted felons were executed, a very great percentage of whom were guilty of the crime of homicide. During the same year, 7,020 criminal homicides were reported.

A decade later, the number of executions dropped to 56, and the number of criminal homicides rose to 9,140.

Throughout the 1960s, we experienced a steady increase in the number of criminal homicides, with 14,590 recorded in 1969. During the same decade, we saw a practical end to the utilization of the death penalty. Since 1967, no executions have occurred in the United States, and there were only two that year. In 1966, there was only one instance in which this form of punishment was applied.

I realize that a very great number of factors are involved in this extremely complex question, and I do not suggest for a moment that the de facto end of the death penalty as a form of punishment is solely responsible for the burgeoning homicide rate in the United States. But I suggest it is equally unrealistic to assume that there is no relationship between the two.

The danger of resorting solely to statistics in attempting to determine the best course of action to follow in something as complex as the issue of the death penalty is illustrated by some of the statistics cited to support its abolition.

Opponents of capital punishment point to the criminal homicide rates in states which have legally banned the death penalty, and claim support for their beliefs in that fact that the statistics in these states are lower than in some in which capital punishment continues to be legally permissible.

The questionable nature of such statistics becomes immediately apparent when we realize that capital punishment as a practical matter has ceased to exist in all states. When four years pass without a single state exacting the death penalty, then statistics comparing states with capital punishment and those without become ridiculous.

We have in effect become a nation in which capital punishment does not exist, and I am convinced that part of the results of this has been a very great increase in capital offenses.

It is equally as invalid to rely on emotional appeals, because there is an inherent element of emotion both in appeals to continue and to discontinue capital punishment.

Lurid descriptions of the death scene have painted a horrible picture of the execution. Of equal impact are descriptions of the savage atrocities visited upon innocent victims by those who commit murders and rapes. A description of the execution scene which revolts and repels is no more valid a basis upon which to make a decision than is the gore of the criminal homicide scene.

Our courts, with every justification, have refused to admit into evidence in the trial of an accused pictures and oral descriptions which repel human sensibilities and are revolting to human decency. The courts realize that reliance upon such methods cause conclusions to be reached on the basis of emotion rather than on the basis of logic.

Such an application can with equal validity be made to execution.

At one time in the history of man, 168 violations were capital offenses. It is to the credit of our forebears that they realized that the death penalty could not properly be applied in minor cases, but must be reserved to those cases of greatest magnitude.

I am convinced that an equal exercise of good judgment calls upon us to decide that conditions can exist in which this act of the utmost gravity is not only justified but is demanded, and that violations can be committed which are so reprehensible that no other form of punishment is suitable.

If we are to apply those methods which serve as the greatest deterrent, we are going to have to continue to suit the punishment to the offense.

The nation's police officers are particularly concerned

This introduction leads into an area that I think is of tremendous concern at the present time because of the near-sighted and one-dimensional drive by those people who don't think this matter through, or who have had no experience with the seamy side of human nature, and who are trying to paralyze what weapons are left to control the law-breakers and to guarantee the freedoms of all. So this leads into a discussion of the victims of serious crimes.

Many criminals escape punishment; none of their victims ever do.

The public is treated to bales of propaganda to bring sympathy for murderers, but never a kind word for their victims.

For example, George Robert Brown was convicted fourteen years ago and sentenced to death for murdering Mildred Grigonis, a Gary beautician; Emmett O. Hashfield was convicted in Boonville in 1962 for the dismemberment slaying of Avril Terry; J. L. Dull was convicted in 1961 for the robbery slaying of taxi-cab driver James L. Tricker of Muncie; Luciano Monserrate was convicted in 1967 for the rape-slaying of Sharon Potts, a hospital clerk at East Chicago; Charles Adams was convicted in 1968 for the slaying of Burl Lyles of Huntington; Paul T. Kennedy was convicted in 1969 for the slaying of Porter County Deputy Sheriff Paul Blakely; Michael T. Callahan of Indianapolis was convicted for slaying Marion County Deputy Sheriff Edward Byrne in 1962. Duly tried and convicted, all seven murderers have thus far avoided their penalties.

Every time the propaganda gushes forth to relieve these murderers and others of their punishment, it might be well if the press would give equal space to the story of the crime and the victim and pictures of the victim before and after the crime.

The purpose of our system of criminal law is to minimize the quantity of human suffering by maintaining a framework of order and peace. The primary object of the law in this area is to forestall acts of violence or other aggression

by which one person inflicts harm on another. To the extent that government fails to do this, the primary function of the State is neglected, and individual suffering is increased.

The question we must ask ourselves about the death penalty is: Which of several possible courses of action will serve the true humanitarian purposes of the criminal law. We must weigh the execution of the convicted murderer against the loss of life of his victims and of the possible victims of other potential murderers.

Many factors enter into the perpetration of crime, some of which are obviously beyond the bounds of social control. And, it is true that some murders occur under circumstances which no system of penalties can prevent. Yet the objective, statistical evidence available to all, indicates one major factor in the commission of crime is the relative probability of punishment *or* escape. If punishment is certain, the impulse to crime is to some extent checked. If escape seems probable, the criminal impulse has freer reign.

The propaganda drive to abolish capital punishment appears to be a geared part of a general drive toward leniency in the treatment of criminals in our society. Such leniency has, in my opinion, had undeniable psychological impact on potential murderers, and has contributed to the upward spiral of the crime rate. There is a striking overall correlation between the recent decline in the use of the death penalty and the rise in violent crime. Such crime has increased by geometric proportions.

In the first three years of the last decade, the number of executions in the United States was by present standards relatively high. Fifty-six persons were executed in 1960; 42 in 1961; and 47 in 1962. During these same three years the number of people who died violently at the hands of criminals actually declined and the murder rate per 100,000 of population also declined.

Beginning in 1963, however, there was a drop in the number of legal executions, and the graph line of violent

crime simultaneously began moving up instead of down. In the following years, the number of legal executions has decreased dramatically from one year to the next, until in 1968 there was none at all. But each of these years has seen murders increase sharply both in absolute numbers and as a percentage of population.

In 1964, for example, the number of legal executions dropped to 15. Yet the number of violent deaths moved up from 8,500 to 9,250, and the murder rate per 100,000 went up from 4.5 to 4.8. In 1965, the number of legal executions dropped to 7, while the number of violent deaths increased to 9,850, and the murder rate went to 5.1 Similar decreases in legal executions have occurred in the following years accompanied by similar increases in the murder rate.

In 1968, with no legal executions at all, the total number who died through criminal violence reached 13,650, while the murder rate climbed to 6.8 per 100,000.

The movement in these figures, with murders increasing as the deterrence of the death penalty diminished, confirms the verdict of ordinary logic: That a relaxation in the severity and certainty of punishment leads only to an increase in crime.

These remarks concern the deterrent effect of the death penalty on those who might commit murder but do not. That is a negative phenomenon which can be inferred both from the record and the assessment of common sense. The repeal of the death penalty would not repeal human nature. To these truisms we may add the fact that there are numerous cases on record in which criminals have escaped the capital penalty for previous murders and gone on to commit others.

Likewise there are numerous cases of prison inmates who have killed guards and other inmates, knowing that the worst punishment they could get would be continued tenancy in the same institution. Opponents of the death penalty usually resist even life sentences without parole, and the deterrent function of that would be even less effective than capital punishment.

The general growth of violent crime in the past decade is the out-cropping of the attitude of permissiveness and leniency going hand-in-hand with an increase in the rate of victimization. As more and more loopholes have been devised for defendants, the crime rate has increased steeply. Between 1960 and 1968, the overall crime rate in America increased 11 times as fast as the rate of population growth —plainly meaning that more and more people are being subjected every day of every year to major personal crimes— murder, rape, assault, kidnapping, armed robbery, etc.

Is a course of action humanitarian which actually encourages a vast and continuing increase in the number of people killed and maimed and otherwise brutalized? There have been many sentimental journeys into the psychological realm of the criminals who are to be executed; I think there should be more sympathetic concern expressed for the thousands of innocent victims of those criminals.

Opponents of the death penalty may rejoice that in 1968 there were 47 fewer murderers executed in this country than was the case in 1962. But do they say anything of the fact that some 5,250 more innocent persons died by criminal violence in 1968 than was the case in 1962?

In the equation of human suffering, this is a staggering loss of more than five thousand individual innocent lives. What about the human rights and civil rights of the individual victim? Are not those five thousand persons entitled to the dignity and sacredness of life? Is that a result of which humanitarians can be proud? I think not.

Only misguided emotionalism, and not facts, dispute the truth that the death penalty is a deterrent to capital crime.

Individuals must be held responsible for their individual actions if a free society is to endure.

BRING BACK THE DEATH PENALTY?[5]

Reprinted from *U.S. News & World Report.*

YES—"THE ONLY PENALTY AVAILABLE THAT COULD POSSIBLY DETER"—*Ernest van den Haag*

Q. Professor van den Haag, why do you favor the use of the death penalty?

A. For certain kinds of crimes it is indispensable.

Thus: The federal prisons now have custody of a man sentenced to life imprisonment who, since he has been in prison, has committed three more murders on three separate occasions—both of prison guards and inmates. There is no further punishment that he can receive. In effect, he has a license to murder.

Take another case: When a man is threatened with life imprisonment for a crime he has already committed, what reason has he not to kill the arresting officer in an attempt to escape? His punishment would be the same.

In short, there are many cases where the death penalty is the only penalty available that could possibly deter.

I'll go a step further. I hold life sacred. Because I hold it sacred, I feel that anyone who takes someone else's life should know that thereby he forsakes his own and does not just suffer an inconvenience about being put into prison for some time.

Q. Could the same effect be achieved by putting the criminal in prison for life?

A. At present, "life imprisonment" means anything from six months—after which the parole board in Florida can release the man—to twelve years in some states. But even if it were real life imprisonment, its deterrent effect will never be as great as that of the death penalty. The death penalty is the only actually irrevocable penalty. Because of

[5] Interviews with Ernest van den Haag and Louis B. Schwartz in *U.S. News & World Report.* 80:37-8. Ap. '76. Professor van den Haag is a psychoanalyst and adjunct professor at New York University; Professor Schwartz is at the Law School of the University of Pennsylvania.

that, it is the one that people fear most. And because it is feared most, it is the one that is most likely to deter.

Recent Analyses of Effects

Q. Authorities seem to differ as to whether the death sentence really does deter crime—

A. Usually the statistics quoted were compiled more than ten years ago and seem to indicate that the absence or presence of the death penalty made no difference in murder rates.

However, in the last ten years there have been additional investigations. The results indicate, according to Isaac Ehrlich's recent article ["Deterrent Effect of Capital Punishment] in the *American Economic Review*: Over the period 1933 to 1969, "an additional execution per year . . . may have resulted on the average in seven or eight fewer murders." [For further analysis of recent articles, see "The Continuing Controversy," by Professor J. Q. Wilson, in this section, below.]

In New York in the last six years, the murder rate went up by 60 percent. Previous to the abolition of the death penalty, about 80 percent of all murders committed in New York were so-called crimes of passion, defined as crimes in which the victim and the murderer were in some way involved with each other. Right now, only 50 percent of all murders in New York are crimes of passion.

Q. How do you interpret those figures?

A. As long as the death penalty existed, largely only people in the grip of passion could not be deterred by the threat of the death penalty. Now that there's no death penalty, people who previously were deterred—who are not in the grip of passion—are no longer deterred from committing murder for the sake of gain. Murder is no longer an irrational act, least of all for juveniles for whom it means at most a few months of inconvenience.

Even if you assume the evidence for the deterrent effect of the death penalty is not clear—I make this point in my book *Punishing Criminals*—you have two risks. Risk 1: If you impose the death penalty and it doesn't have an additional deterrent effect, you have possibly lost the life of a convicted murderer without adding to deterrence and thereby sparing future victims. Risk 2: If you fail to execute the convicted murderer and execution would have had an additional deterrent effect, you have failed to spare the lives of a number of future victims.

Between the two risks, I'd much rather execute the convicted murderer than risk the lives of innocent people who could have been saved.

Q. You noted that the death penalty is irrevocable once it is imposed. Does this make death such a different penalty that it should not be used?

A. It makes it a different penalty. This is why it should be used when the crime is different—so heinous and socially dangerous to call for this extreme measure. When you kill a man with premeditation, you do something very different from stealing from him. I think the punishment should be appropriate. I favor the death penalty as a matter of justice and human dignity even apart from deterrence. The penalty must be appropriate to the seriousness of the crime.

"We Have Cheapened Human Life"

Q. Can you elaborate on your statement that the penalty should match the seriousness of the crime?

A. Our system of punishment is based not just on deterrence but also on what is called "justice"—namely, that we feel a man who has committed a crime must be punished in proportion to the seriousness of the crime. Since the crime that takes a life is irrevocable, so must be the punishment.

All religions that I'm aware of feel that human life is sacred and that its sacredness must be enforced by depriving of life anyone who deprives another person of life. Once we make it clear to a person that if he deprives someone else of life he will suffer only minor inconvenience, we have cheapened human life. We are at that point today.

Q. Some argue that capital punishment tends to brutalize and degrade society. Do you agree?

A. Many of the same people also argue that the death
penalty is legalized murder because it inflicts on the criminal the same situation that he inflicted on his victim. Yet
most punishments inflict on the criminal what he inflicted
on the victim. The difference between the punishment and
the crime is that one is a legal measure and the other is not.

As for brutalizing, I think that people are more brutalized by their daily TV fare. At any rate, people are not so
much brutalized by punishment as they are brutalized by
our failure to seriously punish brutal acts.

No—"Who Is to Decide Who Should Live and Who Should Die?"—*Louis B. Schwartz*

Q. Professor Schwartz, why do you oppose the death
penalty?

A. For a number of reasons. In the first place, mistakes
do occur in our trial system. And, if the victim of a mistake
has been executed, that mistake is irremediable.

For example: I myself once represented a man who had
been frightened into confessing a murder. He was afraid
he'd get the electric chair if he stood trial. So he pleaded
guilty and got life imprisonment. Twelve years later I was
able to prove he was innocent. That would have been too
late if he had been executed.

In the second place—and, for me, very important—the
death penalty, rarely administered as it is, distorts the whole
penal system. It makes the criminal procedure so complex
that it turns the public off.

Q. How does it do that?

A. People are so reluctant to administer the death penalty until every last doubt is eliminated that the procedural
law gets encumbered with a lot of technical rules of evidence. You not only get this in the trial, but you get habeas
corpus proceedings after the trial.

This highly technical procedure is applied not only to capital cases but to other criminal cases as well. So it makes it hard to convict anybody.

I believe the death penalty actually does more harm to security in this country than it does good. Without it, we would be safer from criminals than with it.

Evidence as to Deterrence Inconclusive

Q. Do you think the death penalty is a deterrent to crime?

A. The evidence is inconclusive about that.

The best studies I know, done by Thorsten Sellin, Marvin Wolfgang and their students at the University of Pennsylvania, would indicate that there is no deterrent effect. This study compared states using the death penalty with next-door states that did not use it. They also compared the homicide rates in the same state during periods when it used the death penalty and when it did not. And they found no statistical differences in homicide rates—with or without the death penalty.

I agree that there may be cases where a robber will not shoot because he doesn't want to risk "the hot seat." But, in my opinion, there are also situations where the death penalty stimulates a criminal to kill. I'm talking about cases, for instance, where a kidnapper decides to kill the only witness who could identify him, or where witnesses or informers get wiped out because the criminal says: "If I'm convicted, I'm going to get the chair anyway, and I'm safer if I kill him."

So if the death penalty is not demonstrably helpful in saving innocent lives, I don't think we ought to use it—especially considering the risk of mistakes.

Q. Are there no criminals who commit crimes so heinous that they ought to be executed for society's safety?

A. My view is that society is not well enough organized to make a list of those people who ought to be executed.

Sometimes I think if I were permitted to make up the list of those to be executed I wouldn't mind eliminating some people. But the list that society or the government might make would probably not be the same as my list. Who is to decide who should live and who should die?

Now we're getting to the essential basis of what the Supreme Court must decide. This is whether the processes for choosing the ones to be killed are inevitably irrational, arbitrary and capricious.

Q. Do you think this element of arbitrariness or capriciousness can ever be eliminated—even by making the death penalty mandatory for certain crimes, as many states have?

A. No, I don't. No society has ever been able to make the death-penalty system operate fairly, even by making it mandatory. Look at the British system, which operated for a century with mandatory death penalties. They found juries just wouldn't convict in many cases where the conviction meant execution. And even if the death penalty was imposed, the Home Office eventually decided who would actually be killed by granting or withholding clemency.

Taking human nature as it is, I know of no way of administering a death penalty which would be fair. Not every problem has a solution, you know—and I think this is one of those insoluble problems.

Q. Have we given the death penalty a chance to prove its deterrent effect? It hasn't been applied in this country in recent years—

A. Not just in recent years. Use of the death penalty has been declining for decades. In 1933, there were something like 233 people executed in the United States. Since then, the figures have been going down steadily. And, of course, there haven't been any executions since 1967 because of the litigation over the death penalty's legality. But even before that, the American public was turning against the death penalty.

If you take a poll, you find people overwhelmingly in

favor of the death penalty. But when you ask a person to sit on a jury and vote to execute a defendant, you find a great reluctance—increasingly so in the modern era.

If Judges and Juries Had to Kill—

Q. It has been suggested that jurors and judges who impose a death penalty be required to push the buttons that would carry out the execution—

A. Of course, society would reject that at once. You couldn't get twelve or thirteen people who would do it. They may be willing to vote for it to be done, but they don't want to be a part of it. If you really want to make execution a deterrent, make it public—put it on TV—so people can see what it can be like if they kill someone. But, of course, we won't do that. We keep it hidden away from ourselves.

Q. Do you regard it as immoral to execute a criminal?

A. I steer away from that question because I know people's views on the morality of it are varied—and almost unchangeable. I'm a pragmatist. I just don't think it can be made fair or workable.

DEATH PENALTY [6]

In response to the 1972 Supreme Court ruling on capital punishment, which struck down existing laws as leading to cruel and unusual punishment because of the random way in which they were applied, thirty-five states enacted new legislation designed to meet the constitutional criteria inferable from the Court's 1972 language. By one estimate, 527 individuals are now on Death Row after conviction under these new laws, the constitutionality of which is now under challenge.

In arguing the case for the death penalty before the

[6] Article in *National Review.* 28:437-8. Ap. 30, '76. Reprinted by permission of *National Review*, 150 E. 35th St., New York, NY 10016. (subscription $19 per year)

Court, Mr. Robert Bork, the Solicitor General, stressed two
principal arguments: (a) that capital punishment is a necessary deterrent; and (b) that important questions of social
policy should be settled according to the deliberate sense of
the people as reflected in their legislatures. "Ultimately,"
argued Bork, "these are cases about democratic government."

The familiar argument from deterrence may well be
valid; indeed, it has recently received impressive statistical
support from the work of Chicago economist Isaac Ehrlich.
To be entirely satisfactory, however, it must be comple-
mented by a more central argument from the principle of
justice. Deterring *other* crimes, a laudable enough social
goal, remains entirely utilitarian and, moreover, has nothing
to do with *this* crime, which has already been committed.

The point should be stressed that if the nexus between
crime and punishment is severed by an exclusive reliance
upon the utilitarian argument from deterrence, then no
principled impediment exists to some far-reaching modes
of deterrence indeed. Thus, certain categories of individuals
are statistically more likely to commit crimes of violence
than others. By eliminating such people entirely you could
deter much crime. What stands in the way of such far-reaching social engineering is the idea of justice: it would be un-
just to afflict the innocent merely on the grounds of utilitarian principle.

The idea of punishment-as-just-desert has been widely
denigrated as barbaric, atavistic, mere "revenge." In fact,
the idea of punishment-as-deterrent, standing alone, strips
the individual of his right to justice and turns him into an
object, a mere social lever with which to influence the behavior of others. Far from being "barbaric," therefore, the
older idea of justice-as-desert is profoundly connected with
the idea of civilization. Perhaps it should not be surprising, then, that justice-as-desert has become anathema to the
"modern" mind.

The central question as regards capital punishment thus

becomes one of whether murder, or murder under some circumstances, *deserves* execution. Prolonged meditation on the current bestseller *Helter-Skelter,* prosecutor Vincent Bugliosi's account of the Manson murders, should go far toward answering that question.

THE CONTINUING CONTROVERSY [7]

The death penalty can be defended or criticized on grounds of either justice or utility. By *justice* I mean considerations of fitness and fairness: Death either is or is not a fitting, appropriate or necessary punishment for those who commit certain kinds of crimes, and such punishment either can or cannot be fairly administered. The Biblical injunction, "an eye for an eye," is an argument for death (or at least maiming) on grounds of justice; so also is the argument that the supreme penalty is the only appropriate response to the supreme crime, that we cheapen the value of human life if an innocent victim dies while his convicted murderer lives.

Appeals to justice can also be used to argue for the abolition of the death penalty. Human life is sacred and may never be taken deliberately, even by the state. Further, society ought not to encourage sentiments of vengeance or cater to morbid interest in ritual executions. Moreover, no penalty is acceptable if it is administered in ways that are grossly unfair; in this country, at least, certain disadvantaged groups have experienced a disproportionate number of executions.

The argument on grounds of justice is certainly the most profound and to me the most interesting. As I shall suggest in the course of this discussion, it may be the *only* proper basis for a decision. And at one time, discussion of capital punishment was often based entirely on considerations of justice and morality. The most striking aspect of contem-

[7] From "The Death Penalty," by James Q. Wilson, Shattuck Professor of Government, Harvard University. New York *Times Magazine.* p 26-7+. O. 28, '73. © 1973 by The New York Times Company. Reprinted by permission.

porary discussions of this issue, however, is that, except for
the fairness question, they almost never proceed along moral
lines. And for opponents of capital punishment, the asser-
tion that it is imposed unfairly seems their weakest argument, for it might be answered by making executions mandatory for those convicted of the relevant crimes. This was
the case in England, for example, where, until hanging was
abolished, the judge was required to sentence to death *any*
person convicted of murder (all murder was the same, there
being no distinction, as here, between first and second
degree homicide).

Perhaps because we find it hard to argue about first
principles, perhaps because our leaders and spokesmen are
untrained in the discipline of philosophic discourse, perhaps because we are an increasingly secular and positivist
society that has little confidence in its ethical premises, the
capital punishment debate has been framed largely in utilitarian terms. Most of the literature, in short, does not explore the moral worth or evil of execution so much as the
consequences of executions for other parties, or for society
at large. The utility of capital punishment can depend on
several considerations: Executions are cheaper than confine-
ment in prison for long terms; an executed man cannot
commit additional crimes, and executions deter others from
committing certain crimes. The first two utilitarian reasons
are rarely taken seriously: We usually assume that cost
(within reason) should make no difference when a human
life is at stake and that life imprisonment can prevent the
convicted person from committing additional crimes as
surely as execution. (In fact, of course, the alternative to
execution is not often, or even usually, life imprisonment,
but in many states a life *sentence* with eligibility for parole
in seven, ten or fifteen years. Furthermore, prison may protect society against convicts, but it often does not protect
convicts from each other.)

Though it need not be so, the utilitarian argument is in
practice an argument over deterrence, and deterrence is not

a simple issue. This may be illustrated, to begin with, by considering the problem of placing the burden of proof. Proponents of the death penalty claim that those who favor its abolition must show that it does *not* deter criminals, while opponents argue that those who defend capital punishment must prove that it *does* have a deterrent effect. In one of the better debates, sociologist Ernest van den Haag and Hugo Adam Bedau, professor of philosophy at Tufts University, faced this issue squarely. . . . Van den Haag argued that the burden of proof should fall on the abolitionists. He admitted that society faces the risk of executing persons even though the executions might not deter any potential murderer—or at least would not deter him more than would the possibility of life imprisonment. But he pointed out that society also faces the risk of not executing a convicted murderer when such executions would in fact have deterred other murderers. The choice, he argued, is not between a safe course of action and a risky one, but between two risky ones. For van den Haag, the risk of allowing future innocent victims to be killed by murderers who would have been deterred by capital punishment was far graver than the risk of executing a convicted murderer whose death deters no one. Since the cost to society is greater if we wrongly reject the deterrence theory than if we wrongly accept it, he concluded, those who favor rejecting it ought to be required to prove that it doesn't work.

Bedau saw the matter quite differently. . . . He argued (and up to a point van den Haag would agree) that the issue is not whether the death penalty deters would-be murderers, but whether it deters them more than the prospect of life imprisonment. It is a matter of dispute whether *any* penalty will have a deterrent effect on murderers, but surely the prospect of a long prison term will have as much as most others. For the death penalty to be warranted, it would have to supply an additional increment of deterrence sufficient to offset the costs of imposing it, those costs being the risk of executing an innocent man, the opportunities for discrimination in imposing the penalty, and the forgone possibility of rehabilitating the murderer. Fairness would always be a problem, he notes, because, though imposition of the death penalty could be made mandatory, juries in such cases might be unwilling to convict at all for fear of convicting wrongly.

Here it is interesting to note that in Great Britain, where judges had less discretion in imposing the death penalty than they do in the United States, the number of murderers found insane—and so spared the gallows— dropped sharply after the death penalty was abolished in 1965. It is hard to believe that there were fewer insane persons in Britain after abolition of the death penalty; what apparently happened was that the authorities no longer felt it as necessary to protect the accused from penalties when the penalty was no longer death. No one should assume that any judicial outcome can be made truly "mandatory"—discretion removed from one place in the criminal justice system tends to reappear elsewhere in it.

However academic it may seem, such a debate is useful in that it reveals to us that we can make proper judgments about deterrence only if we have first come to some firm conclusions about the costs and benefits of executions. But the scholarship to date shows that such conclusions are elusive.

The chief cost of the death penalty is thought to be the possibility of erroneously executing an innocent man. But even as ardent an abolitionist as Bedau does not claim that we have paid that cost very often. In 1962, he compiled a list of 74 cases since 1893 in which a wrongful conviction for murder is alleged to have occurred in this country. No one should assume that this is a complete list, but it includes all that until then had been turned up. In only 8 of the 74 cases was the death sentence carried out (there have been more than 7,000 executions in this century); in the majority of cases no death sentence was even imposed. Writing in 1971, Bedau stated that no further instances of erroneous execution had occurred since his earlier review and concluded that it is "false sentimentality to argue that the death penalty should be abolished because of the abstract possibility that an innocent person might be executed, when the record fails to disclose that such cases occur."

The other major cost is the inequity of having certain kinds of persons disproportionately suffer the death penalty. In the North, it is not entirely clear whether certain groups have been unfairly treated. The mere fact that most persons executed are black or poor is not conclusive, since murder occurs disproportionately, for various reasons, among the poor and the black. The best study is probably that of Marvin Wolfgang, professor of sociology at the University of Pennsylvania, and associates in 1962. The 439 persons sentenced to death for murder in Philadelphia between 1914 and 1958 were divided into two categories: those for whom the sentence was commuted and those who were actually executed. Negroes were somewhat more likely than whites to be executed, but the difference, while statistically significant, was not large (88 percent of Negroes, 80 percent of whites were executed). Among those charged with felony murder (that is, with having caused a death that occurs in the course of committing another kind of crime, such as robbery, rape or burglary), whites were three times as likely as blacks to have their sentences commuted. Occupation and social class did not seem to have much effect on one's chances of having his sentence commuted, but having a private lawyer (rather than a court-appointed one) did: Blacks having private counsel were much more likely to get a commutation than blacks having court counsel.

In the South, though, there seems to be fairly strong evidence that blacks, and especially blacks who have murdered or raped a white person, were much more likely than whites, other things being equal, to be sentenced to death.

The most comprehensive study of southern practices is that of Wolfgang and Professor Anthony Amsterdam of the University of Pennsylvania Law School. They examined more than three thousand rape convictions in eleven southern states between 1945 and 1965. They found that a black convicted of rape was not likely to be executed (only 13 percent were) but that blacks were almost 7 times as likely to be executed as whites convicted of the same crime. And if the black had raped a white woman, he was 18 times as likely to be executed as all other racial combinations of criminals and victims. These findings could not be explained away by any other circumstances of the crime. One assumes that in parts of the South, heavier penalties for blacks may be common for many offenses and not just those punishable by death.

If the problem of fairness does exist, however, the importance of it is not particularly clear. For if capital punishment is to be abolished because it is discriminatory, should not all forms of punishment be abolished because they are discriminatory? The answer the abolitionists would give—though they rarely address the problem—is that we single out the death penalty for special judgment because alternatives (like prison) exist for it, because discrimination in prison terms can in principle be corrected by subsequent review and commutation and because, while we may be powerless to end discrimination generally, we can at least prevent the worst consequences of it.

If these are the risks, however unclearly they must be considered, what about the benefits of capital punishment?

Here the problem becomes one of measuring its deterrent effects. Three things can be said about recent attempts to do so: (1) There is virtually no serious study that indicates that the death penalty is a deterrent above and beyond imprisonment; (2) none of these studies is sufficiently rigorous to prove beyond dispute the absence of deterrence; and (3) it is most unlikely we shall ever have a study that settles the matter one way or another, for the obstacles in the way of a conclusive study are probably insuperable.

Thorsten Sellin, emeritus professor of sociology at the University of Pennsylvania, has been responsible for the best-known of these studies. He has compared homicide rates in four ways. First, he compared homicide rates between adjacent states with and without the death penalty. The crude rates for homicide in these groups of states appear to be about the same, and to change in the same ways, regardless of whether a state does or does not have the death penalty on the books. Second, he compared homicide rates within states before and after they abolished or restored the death penalty. The rates did not change significantly after the legal status of the penalties changed. Third, he examined homicide rates in those cities where executions occurred and were presumed to have been publicized. There was no difference in the homicide rate before and after the executions. (Similar studies, with similar results, were done by . . . William Graves [and by others]. Indeed, Graves even uncovered evidence in California that led him to speculate that there was an *increase* in the number of homicides on the days immediately preceding an execution.) Finally, Sellin sought to discover whether law enforcement officers were safer from murderous attacks in states with the death penalty than those without it. He found that the rate at which police officers were shot and killed in states that had abolished capital punishment was the same as the rate in states that had retained the death penalty. Donald R. Campion reached the same conclusion after studying the deaths of state police officers.

It is sometimes argued in rejoinder to these findings that while executions may not deter murderers generally, they will help protect prison guards and other inmates from fatal assaults by convicts who "have nothing else to lose." Sellin compiled a list of 59 persons who committed murders in state and federal prisons in 1965. He concluded that it is "visionary" to believe that the death penalty could reduce the "hazards of life in prison." Eleven of the prison murders were found in states without capital punishment and 43 were in states with it. (The other five were in federal prisons.)

All these studies have serious methodological weaknesses, but whether the weaknesses are sufficient to discredit their unanimous conclusion is far from clear. One problem is the degree of comparability of states with and without the death penalty. Sellin tried to "match" states by taking contiguous ones (for example, Michigan, Indiana and Ohio), but of course such states are not really matched at all—they differ not only in the penalty for murder but in many other respects as well, and these other differences may offset any differences resulting from the form of punishment. Statistical techniques more powerful than those used by Sellin in the 1950s are now available with which to control for these other factors, but thus far no one seems to have published a study of the death penalty that employs them.

Another problem lies in the definition of a capital crime. What should be studied is the rate of crimes for which capital punishment is legally possible. In fact I am not aware of any data on "murder rates" that distinguish between those homicides (like first-degree murder) for which death may be a penalty and those (like second-degree murder or non-negligent manslaughter) for which it may not. Sellin's studies compare homicide rates, but no one knows what fraction of those homicides are first-degree murders for which execution is possible, even in the states that retain capital punishment. Furthermore, death has been imposed to punish crimes other than homicides—for example, kidnapping, skyjacking, armed robbery and assault by a life-term prisoner. These are scarcely ever studied, yet they are among the most feared crimes.

Finally, and perhaps most important, it is not clear from many of these studies what is meant by "the death penalty." If what is meant is simply the legal possibility of execution, then "the death penalty" may be more fiction than fact. In many states that have the death penalty on the books, no executions have in fact been carried out for many years. The majority members of a legislative commission in Massachusetts, for example, reported in 1968 that the death penalty is no deterrent to crime, but the minority members pointed out that no one had been executed in the state since 1947, and therefore no one could say whether the legal possibility of execution was or was not a deterrent. Indeed, in 1960, there were only 56 executions in the entire country, more than half of these occurring in the South; in 1965, there were only 7, and there have been no executions since 1967, when there were 2. [The Gilmore execution in January 1977 was the first in ten years.—Ed.] In short, the comparative studies have not distinguished carefully between states that had abolished the death penalty *de jure* and those that had abolished it *de facto*. And even in states that practice the death penalty, the chances of a murderer's being executed have been so small that a rational murderer might well decide to take the risk. There were 8,000 murders in 1960, but only 56 executions; thus, a murderer's chances of being executed were only about 1 in 140. After 1960, the number of executions dropped sharply, thus improving his chances. We have no way of knowing what the deterrent effect of capital punishment would have been in the last decade or two if the odds had been much lower.

So far, then, deterrence studies show that legally abolishing capital punishment in states that had only rarely imposed it does not lead to any increase in homicide, and that states that rarely execute murderers do not have any more murders than states that never do. The crucial question, at least for those debating the deterrence issue, is whether we can ever say any more than this.

I suspect that we will not be able to say much more. Such factors as region (the South has proportionately more murders than the North), race (blacks are more likely to murder, and to be murdered, than whites) and class (the poor are more likely to murder, and to be murdered, than the well-to-do) all contribute to the homicide rate. If these factors are taken into account in any statistical explanation of the murder rate, the additional importance of the death penalty, or its absence, to the analysis is likely to be slight.

Perhaps the only way to settle the matter would be by experiment—execute all the murderers in a random group of states, imprison all murderers in another random group and observe the results over time. But such a thought serves only to illustrate the happy fact that the social sciences are rarely permitted the carefully controlled procedures of the physical sciences.

Some persons have tried to get at the question of deterrence by simply asking people whether they have been deterred. For example, one could ask criminals, or would-be criminals, how they perceived the consequences of acts they had committed or considered committing. These studies are at best inconclusive, at worst silly. The commonest rely on the testimonies of prison wardens—former Warden Clinton Duffy of San Quentin, for example, who stated that the electric chair, or even prison itself, constitutes no deterrent because the "convicts have told me so again and again." But obviously those *in* prison, or *facing* electrocution, have not been deterred; if they had, they wouldn't be there to talk to the warden. Their statements say nothing about how many nonprisoners may have been deterred.

Another example of this approach was a survey conducted in 1971 by the Los Angeles Police Department. Persons arrested for violent crimes were interviewed to find out whether they were armed and, if not, why not. Of the ninety-nine individuals who either carried no weapon or carried one they did not use, half said that they had been deterred from using a gun by fear of the death penalty. (At this time, California had 94 persons in prison under sentence of death, but only 2 had actually been executed since 1962.) It is as hard to give credence to the views of arrested criminals as to those of myopic wardens. Prisoners in the hands of the police are likely to tell the police what they think they want to hear, and the police are disproportionately inclined to favor the death penalty. Furthermore, even if the data are correct, the best they show is that some people, *under the mistaken belief* that they might be executed, are reluctant to use guns in crimes.

The problem of deterrence has also been considered in light of the nature of murder and murderers. Franklin E. Zimring of the University of Chicago, in a detailed study of assault cases, has shown that sociologically, and probably also psychologically, assault and murder are indistinguishable events in a large proportion of the crimes—most murders are merely "successful" assaults. A typical assault is an encounter between persons known or related to each other in which rage, often stimulated by alcohol or sexual jealousy, leads to violence. Whether the violence leads to murder will often depend, Zimring has shown, on whether or not a weapon is present, and if present, whether it is a knife, a small-caliber gun or a large-caliber gun.

Such crimes of passion are not, as some claim, undeterrable. Even enraged persons are aware that their acts have some consequences, and it seems safe to assume that many more barroom or bedroom fights would end with a weapon being used if there were no penalty at all for the offense. But whether the additional increment of deterrence provided by a death penalty would be significant is far from clear, especially since we have not had in this country and will not have in the future a criminal justice system that imposes death in more than a tiny fraction of homicides of this nature. It might be more useful, Zimring implies, to impose penalties in assault cases whose severity depends on the caliber of the weapon employed. Perhaps we should treat all kinds of assaults more seriously than we do now, instead of waiting until murder results. (An assault arising out of a domestic disturbance is likely to receive virtually no penalty at all under present circumstances.) By raising the price of cuttings and shootings, we might lower the incidence of these murders of passion. Indeed, basing penalties for assaults in part on the kind of weapon (if any) used might contribute more to gun control than passing unenforceable laws calling for civilian disarmament.

But what about murderers who exhibit a degree of calculation and premeditation? There are three kinds—the cold-blooded killer who intends and carefully contrives his victim's death, the maniacal killer who is irrational in every sense except his ability to arrange another person's demise and the robber or arsonist who plots a property crime that results in the death of another person, with or without his intending it. The professional, the compulsive and the felon murderer (or their counterparts in other major crimes, such as espionage, kidnapping or hijacking) are the principal candidates for the death penalty. The criminal justice system already recognizes this: Setting aside the compulsive, who may be judged criminally insane and thus institutionalized, the courts impose especially severe penalties on professional, felon or other calculating murderers such as assassins, terrorists and kidnappers.

There is no evidence whatsoever to indicate whether the state's power to punish such persons with death will or will not reduce the probability of these crimes. If the public and their elected officials are to make decisions on this matter, as they must, they will have to rely on their own best judgment. "Best judgment" means two things: how one thinks people will react to certain penalties and whether one thinks such penalities are fair and just. Social science can do little more than rule out certain sweeping generalizations, such as that "we can prove that the death penalty deters."

If public opinion is to play a role in these matters, what can we expect of it? In 1964, the citizens of Oregon voted in a referendum to abolish the death penalty in that state, but in 1966, Colorado voters chose to retain its death penalty statute, as did the voters in Illinois in 1970. In a nonbinding referendum in 1968, Massachusetts voters expressed the view that they favored keeping capital punishment. These referenda were all broadly phrased, of course, and even if one accepts the results, they do not settle such issues as the circumstances under which death might be imposed.

Gallup polls taken over several years indicate that support for the death penalty declined from 68 percent in 1953 to 42 percent in 1966. In that year, a majority of those interviewed would have repealed the death penalty for murder. Perhaps because of the rise in crime rates during the late 1960s, support for capital punishment has gone up again slightly. In 1969, 51 percent said they favored it. Young persons are more opposed to death penalties than older ones and women more than men. Somewhat surprisingly, the better-educated and higher-income respondents are not much more opposed to it than those with less education or income. As Hugo Bedau put it, there is little evidence in the polls that the death penalty is more favored by the "hard hats" than by the professional classes.

Given the fact that blacks are disproportionately the victims of murder, one might suppose that they would favor the death penalty. But quite the opposite is the case. Hans Zeisel reports survey data indicating that only a third of black men, but over half of white men, favor capital punishment. Black women are even less inclined to support the death penalty.

People often adapt their views to support whatever state of affairs happens to exist, and attitudes toward the death penalty may be no exception. Until the Supreme Court decision, California had the death penalty, and almost two-thirds of those polled in that state said they favored its retention. Minnesota has not had the death penalty since the early part of this century, and two-thirds of those polled in that state said they opposed restoring it.

These changes in attitude have been accompanied, over the years, by a trend to greater respect for human life and a tendency to regard execution as somehow barbaric, even if necessary. A hundred years ago a large crowd would turn

out for a public hanging; today, public opinion only barely
supports executions at all, and a large majority would probably condemn its being a public spectacle. A hundred and
fifty years ago, a large number of offenses were punishable
by death; today, scarcely anyone regards it as remarkable
that in general only murder is considered a sufficiently
grave crime to warrant the thought of capital punishment.
One of the striking facts about the [1972] Supreme Court
decision . . . is that, although only a bare five-man majority
found the death penalty as administered to be unconstitutional, eight of the nine Justices indicated their personal
opposition to it.

The main issue remains that of justice—the point is not
whether capital punishment prevents future crimes, but
whether it is a proper and fitting penalty for crimes that
have occurred. That is probably as it should be, for such a
question forces us to weigh the value we attach to human
life against the horror in which we hold a heinous crime.
Both that value and that horror change over time. In our
modern culture we seem to be uncomfortable about considering these matters, and thus both proponents and opponents of execution fall back on "scientific" assertions
about deterrence that are not only dubious but are likely
to remain so. The quality of public debate would be sub-
stantially improved if all sides recognized this.

BIBLIOGRAPHY

An asterisk (*) preceding a reference indicates that the article or a part of it has been reprinted in this book.

BOOKS, PAMPHLETS AND DOCUMENTS

*Bedau, H. A. ed. The death penalty in America; an anthology. rev ed Doubleday. '67.

Bedau, H. A. and Pierce, C. M. eds. Capital punishment in the U.S. AMS Press. '76.

Black, C. L. jr. Capital punishment; the inevitability of caprice and mistake. Norton. '74.

Bowers, W. J. Executions in America. Lexington Books. '74.

*Clark, Ramsey. Crime in America. Simon & Schuster. '70; Pocket Books. '71.

DiSalle, M. V. and Blochman, L. G. The power of life or death. Random House. '65.

Heline, Theodore. Capital punishment: historic trends toward its abolishment. New Age. '65.

Horwitz, E. L. Capital punishment, U.S.A. Lippincott. '73.

Joyce, J. A. Capital punishment: a world view. T. Nelson. '61.

McCafferty, J. A. ed. Capital punishment. (Controversy series) Aldine. '72.

McClellan, G. S. ed. Capital punishment. (Reference Shelf, v 32, no 6) Wilson. '61.

Neier, Aryeh. Crime and punishment; a radical solution. Stein and Day. '76.

Roucek, J. S. Capital punishment; ed. by D. S. Rahmas. (Topics of Our Times series) new ed Sam Har Press. '75.

Sellin, J. T. ed. Capital punishment. Harper. '67.

United Nations. Department of Economic and Social Affairs. Capital punishment; developments 1961-1965; prepared by Marc Ancel. United Nations. '67.

Van den Haag, Ernest. Punishing criminals. Basic Books. '75.

PERIODICALS

America. 124:501. My. 15, '71. Due process and the death penalty.

America. 127:55-9. Ag. 5, '72. California views the death penalty. M. E. Leary.

*America. 135:410-12. D. 11, '76. Terrorism and the death penalty. T. P. Thornton.

American Economic Review. 65:397-417. Je. '75. Deterrent effect of capital punishment: a question of life and death. Isaac Ehrlich.

American West. 7:11. Ja. '70. Collector's choice: a first for law & order [execution of José Forner in San Francisco]. Roger Olmsted.

Annals of the American Academy of Political and Social Science. 407:119-33. My. '73. Race, judicial discretion and the death penalty. M. E. Wolfgang and Marc Riedel.

Business Week. p 92+. S. 15, '75. Crime: a case for more punishment. Isaac Ehrlich.

Christian Century. 88:1044. S. 8, '71. Church groups file brief against death penalty.

Christian Century. 90:99-101. Ja. 24, '73. Immorality of the death penalty. D. R. Burrill.

Christian Century. 90:333. Mr. 21, '73. Death penalty for terrorists?

Christian Century. 90:468-9. Ap. 25, '73. Life without the hangman. T. R. Beeson.

Christian Century. 92:483-4. My. 14, '75. Capital punishment: a moral consensus? J. M. Wall.

*Christian Century. 93:60-2. Ja. 28, '76. British and the IRA. Trevor Beeson.

Christian Century. 93:653-5. Jl. 21, '76. Green Haven prison and the death sentence. C. M. Robinson.

Christianity Today. 14:37. Ja. 16, '70. Hanging is dead in Britain.

Christianity Today. 19:10-12+. My. 23, '75. Restoring the death penalty: proceed with caution. Dave Llewellyn.

Commonweal. 98:127+. Ap. 13, '73. One vote for the hangman. Peter Steinfels.

Commonweal. 100:107-8. Ap. 5, '74. Children of Cain? Senate vote and Harold Hughes' amendment. Sisyphus, pseud.

Commonweal. 103:518-19. Ag. 13, '76. Bringing back death: Supreme Court decisions. R. A. Pugsley.

*Congressional Digest. 52:1-32. Ja. '73. Controversy over the question of capital punishment in the U.S.
    Excerpts reprinted in this book: Capital punishment in the U.S.: facts and figures. p 2-4; In the interest of life. G. D. King. p 15+.

Current History. 71:14-18+. Jl. '76. The problem of capital punishment. H. A. Bedau.

*Daily News. p 45. Ja. 6, '77. Slavery triggers two trips to gallows. Paul Meskil.

*Daily News. p 39. Ja. 7, '77. How the electric chair changed executions. Paul Meskil.

Esquire. 75:179-80. Ap. '71. Death by degrees. R. L. Massie.

Good Housekeeping. 169:24+. N. '69. Should capital punishment be revived? [Good Housekeeping poll]

Intellect. 103:281. F. '75. Mandatory death sentences.

Nation. 212:48-50. Ja. 11, '71. Primitive relic: death sentence. Elmer Gertz.

Nation. 212:610. My. 17, '71. Ultimate question.

Nation. 212:772-3. Je. 21, '71. Act of mercy; Senator Hart's proposal.

Nation. 215:548-9. D. 4, '72. Voting their fears. M. E. Leary.

Nation. 217:356-7. O. 15, '73. Death row returns.

Nation. 220:612-13. My. 24, '75. Still cruel and unusual: arguments on capital punishment before the Court. H. A. Bedau.

Nation. 222:37-8. Ja. 17, '76. Death as a cover-up? T. E. Gaddis.

*Nation. 223:144-8. Ag. 28, '76. New life for the death penalty. H. A. Bedau.

National Review. 21:384-5+. Ap. 22, '69. Capital punishment: has it become cruel and unusual? A. W. Green.

National Review. 23:1351-4. D. 3, '71. Wistful goodbye to capital punishment. D. A. Zoll.

*National Review. 28:437-8. Ap. 30, '76. Death penalty.

Nation's Business. 58:28. N. '70. Matter of life or death.

Nation's Business. 61:20-1. Ap. '73. Resounding vote for the death penalty.

New Republic. 164:12. F. 20, '71. Death to capital punishment.

New Republic. 167:7-8. Jl. 15, '72. Mixed reviews; Supreme Court ruling.

New Republic. 168:16. F. 3, '73. Death penalty.

New Republic. 169:12-13. Jl. 21, '73. Capital punishment. Michael Meltsner.

New Republic. 172:17-19. Ap. 19, '75. Give 'em death? Michael Roberts.

New York Times. p 1+. O. 5, '76. Supreme Court ends death penalty ban in cases of murder. Lesley Oelsner.

New York Times. p 22. O. 28, '76. Death penalty a dying law. Tom Goldstein.

*New York Times. p 15. N. 15, '76. Death wish is discerned in poetry and killings by doomed convict. Jon Nordheimer.

New York Times. p 8. D. 10, '76. Confusion reigns as law is in limbo. Tom Goldstein.

*New York Times. p E9. D. 26, '76. A Christmas vigil. Tom Wicker.

*New York Times. p 1+. Ja. 18, '77. Gilmore is executed after stay is upset. Jon Nordheimer.

New York Times. p 21. Ja. 18, '77. Opponents of death penalty fear psychological effects of execution. Tom Goldstein.

New York Times. p 30. Ja. 18, '77. An American punishment again [editorial].

New York Times. p 1+. My. 9, '77. Backers of the death penalty are making scant progress. Douglas Kneeland.

New York Times Magazine. p 46-7+. O. 12, '69. Case that could end capital punishment: Maxwell v. Bishop. Richard Hammer.

*New York Times Magazine. p 26-7+. O. 28, '73. Death penalty; pro and con arguments. J. Q. Wilson.

*New York Times Magazine. p 8+. Ja. 23, '77. The case against capital punishment. Abe Fortas.

Newsweek. 77:23-4+. Ja. 11, '71. Death row: a new kind of suspense.

Newsweek. 77:30-2. My. 17, '71. Question of life or death.

Newsweek. 80:20. Jl. 10, '72. Court on the death penalty.

Newsweek. 81:30+. Je. 11, '73. Bring back the chair; warden and deputy murdered in Holmesburg prison.

Newsweek. 86:31. Jl. 21, '75. Crusading for death: Joe Freeman Britt, district attorney of Lumberton, N.C. J. K. Footlick and Eleanor Clift.

Newsweek. 88:14-15. Jl. 12, '76. Reviving the death penalty: Supreme Court decision. Susan Fraker and Diane Camper.

Newsweek. 88:26-7+. N. 29, '76. Death wish. Peter Goldman and others.

Newsweek. 88:35-6. N. 29, '76. Dusting off "Old Sparky." J. K. Footlick and Lucy Howard.

Progressive. 38:38. My. '74. Waiting on death row: North Carolina. Luisita Lopez.

Progressive. 40:8-9. S. '76. Death delayed; Supreme Court decision.

Psychology Today. 10:16-17. S. '76. Death penalty and public knowledge. Gary Gregg.

Ramparts. 10:42-7. My. '72. Deaths I have known. José Yglesias.

*Saturday Review. 54:28-9. S. 25, '71. Above and beyond capital punishment. George Stevens.

Scientific American. 228:45. Ap. '73. Electricide: first use of the electric chair.

Seventeen. 32:248. Ag. '73. Capital punishment is legalized murder. Alfred Kohn.
Seventeen. 32:248. Ag. '73. Capital punishment is necessary. James Rawitsch.
Time. 97:25. Mr. 15, '71. Bring back "Old Sparky"; opinions of thousands of Texans.
Time. 97:64. My. 17, '71. Fatal decision; Supreme Court on death penalty.
Time. 99:54-5. Ja. 24, '72. Death penalty: cruel and unusual? J. M. Ferrer, 3d.
Time. 100:37. Jl. 10, '72. Closing death row.
Time. 102:94. S. 17, '73. Death killers; cruel and unusual, story behind Supreme Court's abolition of the death penalty.
Time. 104:75. D. 16, '74. Living on death row; inmates of Central prison, Raleigh, N.C. J. E. White.
Time. 105:58+. Ap. 21, '75. Death dealing; case before the Supreme Court.
Time. 107:49. Ap. 12, '76. Reconsidering the death penalty.
Time. 108:35-7. Jl. 12, '76. Death penalty revived: Supreme Court decision.
U.S. News & World Report. 70:26. Ap. 12, '71. Death sentence for Manson clan, but—.
U.S. News & World Report. 70:37-8. My. 31, '71. Signs of an end to death row: U.S. joining trend?
*U.S. News & World Report. 70:38-40. My. 31, '71. Death penalty: a world survey.
U.S. News & World Report. 73:25-7. Jl. 10, '72. End to death row? what Supreme Court ruled.
U.S. News & World Report. 73:60. D. 4, '72. Moves to restore the death penalty.
U.S. News & World Report. 74:70. Mar. 26, '73. Death penalty gets a big push.
U.S. News & World Report. 76:46. Mr. 4, '74. Capital punishment: it's being revived in many states.
U.S. News & World Report. 78:52. Ap. 14, '75. In spite of all the talk of restoring death penalty—. P. R. Oster.
*U.S. News & World Report. 80:37-8. Ap. '76. Bring back the death penalty? pro and con views. Ernest van den Haag; L. B. Schwartz.
*U.S. News & World Report. 81:49-51. Jl. 12, '76. Spreading impact of a historic court decision: death penalty ruling.
*U.S. News & World Report. 81:51-3. Jl. 12, '76. Death-row interviews: five under sentence to die speak out.
U.S. News & World Report. 81:19. N. 29, '76. The questions that are raised when a condemned man wants to die.

Vital Speeches of the Day. 35:273-7. F. 15, '69. Double jeopardy:
    black and poor; address, January 12, 1969. F. H. Williams.
*Vital Speeches of the Day. 37:574-6. Jl. 1, '71. Criminal violence;
    how about the victim? address, May 12, 1971. T. L. Sendak.
Wall Street Journal. p 1+. Ja. 4, '77. For world's alienated vio-
    lence often reaps political recognition. J. A. Tannenbaum.

(383)

with this issue, not merely because they are called upon for direct involvement in the incidents which may result in the application of the death penalty, but because they themselves are so often the victims of offenses for which the death penalty may be assessed. We have in recent years seen a very great increase in the number of criminal assaults committed on the police officer, and in the number of injuries and fatalities resulting from those assaults.

Several of the five states which have partially abolished the death penalty have retained it for the killing of a police officer or a prison or jail guard who is in the performance of his duties. The states of New Mexico, New York, and Vermont have specifically cited such offenses as being justification for the exercise of the death penalty while prohibiting it in other criminal homicides.

Whether these states are correct in their partial abolition of the death penalty, they are unquestionably correct in their implication that the death of a police officer inflicted while that officer is acting in the line of duty is somewhat different and apart from other criminal homicides.

The policeman willingly subjects himself to a greater element of danger than most persons ever experience while protecting the citizens he serves. He is not, however, willing to be the victim of the criminal who uses violence as the method of obtaining that which he seeks. Nor is he willing to be the victim of felonious assault merely because his assailant knows that he can maim and kill without being subjected to meaningful and appropriate punishment.

I am of the belief that capital punishment must be assessed only after every legal safeguard has been provided, and that it can be properly applied only with a full understanding of the very great gravity of its exercise.

But I am convinced, and I urge you to conclude, that capital punishment under carefully prescribed conditions and for highly selective offenses is a deterrent to certain kinds of crimes, and that the value of human life is not

lessened but is rather protected by retention of the death
penalty as a form of punishment.

HOW ABOUT THE VICTIM? [4]

J. Edgar Hoover, . . . [late] director of the Federal
Bureau of Investigation . . . [once] asked this question of
all law enforcement officials: "Who speaks for the victims
of crime in America?" And he . . . [gave] this answer: "Aside
from the weak-muffled cries of the victims themselves, practically no one."

And he . . . [went] on to say:

Are crime victims in the United States today the forgotten
people of our time? Do they receive a full measure of justice? . . .
While many victims are specifically picked by their criminal as-
sailants, others are "chance" targets, ill-fated in being at the
wrong place at the wrong time. No one is immune. As a rule,
when criminal violence strikes, any number of things may happen to the victim. He may be murdered. If not, he may receive
serious injuries, sustain a sizable monetary loss, miss time from
work, incur costly medical and hospital expenses, and suffer un-
told mental anguish. To some degree at least, his right to freedom and the pursuit of happiness is violated.

Meanwhile, if his assailant is apprehended and charged, the
full power of our judicial processes ensues to protect his constitutional rights. This is well and good.

But, how about the victim? Frequently, the compassion he
may receive from the investigating enforcement officers, his family, and his friends is the only concern expressed in his behalf.
Indeed, in some instances the crime victim witnesses organized
campaigns of propaganda to build sympathy for his guilty assailant, campaigns of lies and innuendoes which charge that the
criminal, not the victim or the law-abiding public, is the one who
has been "sinned against." The tragedy is that in some instances
these false claims are repeated and publicized without question
by various means, apparently for no reason other than that those
doing so want to believe the accusations. Consequently, the popular cause legally to protect the criminal is crowding his victim
from beneath the dome of justice.

[4] From "Criminal Violence: How About the Victim?" by Theodore L. Sendak,
former attorney general of Indiana. The address was delivered May 12, 1971, before the luncheon meeting of law enforcement officials of northern Indiana.
Vital Speeches of the Day. 37:574-6. Jl. 1, '76. Reprinted by permission.